Taking
My Hand Out
Of My Pocket

By: Lorie Tensen

IWD
NOW
PUBLISHING

Acknowledgments

Writing this book has been a challenge: an exhausting, painful, soul-searching, yet cathartic challenge. This is my life – my very own personal history in all its beauty and ugliness. I've found myself comparing the writing of this book to being naked in front of strangers, friends and loved ones. It's one thing to stroll naked on a nudist beach filled with strangers on a beach thousands of miles away, however, it's quite another to shed your clothing in front of friends and family ...the horror...the judgments! But here it is – a small tome – basically an outline of the most painful moments in my life that created the woman I am today. It could easily have been a book much longer in length with pages filled with so much more. But these are the most essential moments and I share them with you because I no longer have anything to hide.

Special thanks to my parents: Gerard and Doris Tensen. Dad: I am so grateful that our final words to each other were "I love you". I feel your presence in my life every day and I miss you. Mom: I love you. Period, that's it. This is OUR story – yours and mine. Thanks to my siblings and their children: Mike, Tim and Jody. Family has no color boundary and blood ties are irrelevant when you are a family! Thank you for loving me – just the way I am.

Thank you to the many friends who encouraged me to tell my story – there are too many to name! A special shout-out to Greg, the Mclean family and Jenine who make silly, tacky jokes about my prosthetic, tease me with ease and firmly but, gently re-direct me when necessary because they love me and see beyond the physical.

Finally: thank you most especially to my children – my heart and soul, the lights of my life. Noah and Remington, I love you with every fiber of my being and I am blessed to be your mom. Thank you so much for loving me unconditionally; thank you for showing that love by always being able to open your hearts to accept those who might be a little "different" than the norm in any way, shape, or form. I am so proud of both of you: no matter what path you choose to follow in life, I will always be your champion!

This book is dedicated to my home town: Brooten, Minnesota

Cover photo: Sloan H. Mclean
Videographer: Remington F. P. Wilson

Foreword

She was a college student here Grand Rapids, having just moved here from Minnesota. She was referred to my office because she wore a right below elbow external powered prosthesis. At the time this was a state-of-the-art style prosthesis and prosthetist from Minnesota had referred her to me.

Our first meeting we dealt with her establishing a new person the help her with her prosthesis and the prosthetic needs at the time. I was impressed with a very attractive young lady who had a personality that just seemed limitless.

Over the years while she certainly did work with her prosthetic issues a friendship developed from that initial meeting. I came to know Lorie is a person as in all my patients after you deal with their limb loss you get to know the people. Lorie is a person that that is certainly been affected by limb loss but you quickly get by that portion of her and see how she is like any of us and/or all of us. She has her ups and downs her successes and failures. All the while this lady cannot be limited by what other people think and what other circumstances try to limit her. She is constantly pushing the limits and not afraid to ask what if.

~David Firlik, Mary Free Bed, Orthotics & Prosthetics

My father came home the evening of August 15, 1979 as any other summer evening. He was the manager of the local grain elevator and it was the busy harvest season. I was used to seeing grain dust coated over the brim of his branded feed cap and the shoulders of his western cut shirt. However, on this particular evening he was freshly clean. I had heard a fire siren go off earlier and knew he must have cleaned up either before or after he went out on the call in his role of a volunteer fireman. Dad wanted to speak to my mom privately which didn't matter to me as I was 12, not quite a teenager, but nearing it in only ten days so I felt I was quite mature and ready to enter seventh grade. Our town was small enough that students from kindergarten through sixth grade resided in one building leaving the seventh grade students to start over as the youngest in the high school, a few blocks away, with the rest of the students.

My parent's conversation seemed short when you consider them taking the time to have the formality of speaking alone. I was startled when my dad said "Jen, we need to talk to you." I couldn't imagine that I had done anything wrong and I made a mental note of the chores I had been assigned. Although they could have been more proficiently, I had actually finished everything. I specifically remember my parents looking very tired as the three of us sat at the kitchen table set for four to eat dinner, which was now becoming slightly over-cooked. My dad didn't waste time and said: "there has been an accident." My mind went into a blur as he explained my classmate Lorie had been caught in a piece of equipment to cut meat at her family's grocery store. I don't remember him telling me anything more than the fact she may lose her arm. What he didn't tell me it was he who held her on his lap while others tried to remove the device from her arm. Just one of the volunteer firemen called to rescue the young girl from this inexplicable tragedy.

My first thought was if she lost her arm Lorie wouldn't be able to play the piano. I longed to play the piano as effortlessly as she did. My anxiety would not allow my fingers to glide across the ivory keys in front of an audience. I could play my black upright piano alone in my room, if no one was listening, for hours at a time. But once I knew there were ears tuned in, I shook like a brown leaf holding on to a limb in the November winds. Earlier that spring, Lorie had accompanied me and another classmate on the piano as we sang "Send in the Clowns" for a local talent show. I didn't want to sing, I wanted to play the piano, and what is more ironic is the fact that Lorie's singing voice was even more magical than her touch on keyboard. Yet I sang, she played and a small group of sixth grade girls had the confidence to compete in a talent show with adults. I guess it was because we really didn't know any better.

"Can I visit her?" was the first thing I said when my mind finally cleared.

"In time, yes, you can."

I don't remember if time stood still or moved fast those next days when the town was filled with updates of Lorie's condition and progress. Finally, she was well enough for visitors and our classmate Janet and I went to see her in the hospital in Willmar, MN. A city compared to our small town of Brooten as it had stop lights and a McDonalds.

My mom allowed us to go to a local florist so I could buy Lorie a flower. I knew her preference and I didn't believe the hospital's gift shop would have what I considered the only appropriate gift for Lorie as her tastes were special. I pulled out my babysitting money to purchase a single lavender rose in a white bud vase. I remember the woman telling me that the lavender roses are the most fragrant of all of the rose varieties and actually the red rose has little to no smell. These lavender beauties have remained my favorite rose.

The hospital room was decorated with get well cards; the tables, the walls, there didn't seem to be a bit of the paint that was left exposed. Lorie looked beautiful, but weak wearing a hospital gown and mostly covered with linens. I remember trying to focus on her large brown eyes as we asked how she was doing instead of searching for signs of what was no longer there. Lorie had her right arm behind a large pillow in a starchy white pillowcase. We made uncomfortable small talk, but I did revel in the fact she loved the rose and was so happy I remembered what she liked. At that moment, no one knew if she would be joining our class of 35 for the first day of 7th grade. Thirty-four seemed frightfully small and I didn't want to imagine her not being there.

Our high school career began with Lorie at our side that September. Life went on: Lorie still played the piano, but it was the electric keyboard and she learned to write left handed. Our friendship grew stronger throughout those high school years. We got ready together for our junior prom, sang duets, my alto to her powerful and mesmerizing soprano and took our senior photos together. In the friendship photo we shared, Lorie was wearing a Kelly green jacket with a sporty white polo, me in my bright red jacket and lacy Gunne Sax blouse with the buttons that looked like pearls. We were opposite and yet we had a deep understanding of each other that transcended our looks and general personality traits.

Lorie and I are both adopted which has created yet another unique kinship between the two of us. We share an understanding of how difficult it is to form trusting relationships with others having never experienced those first precious months of bonding with our natural mothers, but rather we were shuffled between various foster homes until we found our way into our adoptive parents' homes and hearts.

From this powerful common place, we have built and maintained a deep friendship although hundreds of miles have separated us through our adult lives. We have shared many joys and losses together: births of our children, deaths of our fathers and unfortunately, the ends of both our marriages. I marveled at Lorie as she became a single parent at such a young age. I was so inspired by her resilience and ability to find joy in life that it continues to help me frame who I want to be, how I want the world to see me.

I see Lorie is as one of the most beautiful women in the world. Physically stunning, while emotionally strong; caring, with the ability to show unconditional love to her children, family and her dearest friends. I am so grateful to be able to be part of her life, to see her journey and now watch as she inspires others as she has for so long inspired me.

God speed Lorie. God speed.

~Jenine Bertsch Keegan

BLACK-EYED SUSABELLE

Most stories are divided into three sections: a beginning, middle and end. However, my story has several beginnings, a bit of a middle section, and the beginning of what I know will be a happy ending. This is the true story of a little girl lost and a little girl found. It is a story of life, quasi-death and rebirth. Most importantly, it is a story of love.

In the beginning that began everything, there was a man and a woman. He was married and she was a single young woman who had immigrated to the United States from Honduras. Together, they created a child. That child was me. The rest of their story is a mystery that perhaps one day I'll solve but, this is my story – not theirs. I was born in St. Paul, Minnesota on May 7, 1966, given the name "Marguerita" and released for adoption immediately upon birth. As I researched statistics on race relations and transracial adoption in the 1960s for informational purposes in relation to my story, I was amazed and quite honestly – thankful – that I had not become a sad statistic of the times. Transracial adoption means: the joining of racially different parents and children together in adoptive families. In the late 1960s, neighborhoods in cities like Chicago, Newark, Omaha, Minneapolis-St. Paul, Washington D.C and Watts (to name a few) were experiencing racial tension and riots. Research shows that black children then – and now –

spend more time as legal orphans than children of any other races. As for children of mixed race, like me, they were to be pitied: neither black nor white, unloved and rootless. Trans-racial placement of children was seen as a last resort, to be used only when a same race placement could not be made. I spent the first seven months of my life living in foster homes, there is no record of how many but, I have read the reports written by the last foster mother and according to her, and I was a happy, healthy baby girl. Upon reflection, I am extremely grateful that my biological female contributor gave me up for adoption. I cannot fathom how my life could have turned out had she not made that difficult decision. So, how exactly did I end up becoming a Minnesota farm girl? My mother has always told me the following story and this is the one I'll stick to. After the adoption of their son, my brother Tim, my parents decided to add one more child to their family. My mother says she was looking through books of children available for adoption at an agency in Glenwood, Minnesota. There were three books: one for white children, one for black children, and one that bore the cringe-worthy title of: "Hard to Adopt Children". During the 1960s, this meant the children who were neither black nor white but biracial or multiracial. My mom says she fell in love with a chubby brown baby girl in one of the pictures and without pointing out to her husband which baby she was determined to have join their family, she handed the book to him and asked him to look through it. My soon-to-be dad paged through the book, looked at the photographs and also fell in love with the picture of the same chubby brown baby girl. The final thumbs-up came from their eldest – and only - natural born child – Mike, who was 12 years old at the time. He too, decided the chubby brown girl was meant to be a part of the family. So, in December of 1966 at the tender age of 7 months, I became the fourth and youngest child in the family of Gerard and Doris Tensen and sibling to Mike, Jody and Tim. I am still awed at the chutzpah this couple had in choosing me – a mixed race child - to be their daughter: they were a white, Dutch, Christian Reformed couple raising their family in an all-white farming community in the Midwest....during a time when cities were burning down all over the United States because of racial tensions. Their willingness put themselves in a position of being subjected to possible disapproval, of not only the community in which they lived but from members of their own families as well, because there were no other people of color within a 300 mile radius. As it happened, there was only one disgruntled relative who readily voiced her disapproval of my joining the family. Suffice it to say, she was overruled and ignored by everyone else. My mother tells me that she would take me shopping at stores out of town and strangers would approach, both fascinated and appalled, and without hesitation, make judgmental comments....even going so far as to hint that my mother must have been fraternizing with a black man. My mother would tartly respond: "Yes, she looks just like her father!" Happily for me, my parents were and are incredibly stubborn and resilient. I am their "Black-eyed Susabelle" and the spoiled one according to my siblings.

My parents raised me to never think of myself as being different than anyone else just because my skin was brown. We rarely – if ever – discussed the color of my skin or the texture of my hair that is...aside from the many times I found myself (quite humorously) the gauge as to whether or not it had been a good summer for tanning - usually by my brothers who would brag smugly that they were darker than me at the end of every summer! On Saturday evenings, Mom would brush, comb and curl my hair into submission so that on Sunday mornings, it would mimic the bouffant hair style of my sister with a little flip in the back. I do have to admit that while living with blinders on was acceptable as a very young, naive child, when I entered school, I knew better: I was different. It was an emotional tug-of-war for me: on the one hand, I was loved and adored by relatives and friends and treated as if I were a cute little doll. I remember quite vividly every time my handsome maternal grandfather would come to visit. He would hand out zebra-striped gum to his grandchildren and knowing that the green pieces were my favorite, would remove them from all of the gum packets he'd brought and give them to me on the sly. My paternal grandfather, usually not the most demonstrative of men, would wrap me in his arms when he greeted me and rub his whiskers on my face – saying he was giving me sugar kisses. In elementary school, the soft, woolly hair that my mother spent countless hours trying to style was stroked and combed so often by curious fingers that on every picture day, the office ladies would have to call her in to school to redo my hair because of the tangled mess. In nearly every one of my elementary school pictures, I am sporting either lop-sided pigtails or two tightly knitted braids. On the other hand, being "different" outside of my community was incredibly uncomfortable and scary. Strangers didn't hesitate (without permission) to touch my body, face and hair– as though my nut brown skin had a different texture than theirs. I began to retreat behind a veil of shyness that became almost physically painful at times. I wanted to tell these strangers to stop touching me, but when you are young and you've not been prepared to appreciate that you do indeed look different than everyone else, how does a child stand up for themselves when they are conflicted in a way they don't yet understand? I was on an already uncomfortable stage that was a sign of things yet to come.

Life in Brooten, Minnesota was simple and fairly bucolic: a small town of 650 residents surrounded by a few hundred farmers and small farms. Main Street was 2 blocks long and there was a bakery, a couple of gas stations, a grainary, a creamery where milk from local farmers was turned into butter, one high school, one elementary school, and several churches. As of 2014, there still wasn't a stop light, despite the increase in population by nearly 100 people! Church picnics were de rigueur and the Bonanza Valley Days parade was the highlight of summer: it featured the reigning Miss Brooten queen and floats from local businesses.

I was raised on a small dairy farm a mile and a half from town. We had a huge garden to weed, with strawberries, sweet corn, onions, potatoes, green beans and a plethora of other vegetables to sell, can and freeze. Various species of animals to feed, cows to milk, fields to plow and sow with corn, soybeans and wheat, and hay to rake and bale. Family reunions were held at beautiful, blue Minnesota lakes and holiday celebrations were deliciously scented with the aromas of homemade pies, cookies and cakes baked by my mother, as well as my grandmothers and aunts. Roasted hams and the occasional goose are happy memories from my childhood made even better by the multitude of cousins available to play kick the can, board games and cards. I took swimming lessons at local lakes during the summer time with an allowance of 15 cents to spend on candy after my lesson and sped over mountains of snow on snowmobiles during the crisp, cold days of winter.

I wasn't a particularly a gregarious child, in fact, I was rather shy – preferring to read books in my hideout above the garage, preach lengthy sermons to the sinful sparrows that gathered on the electric wires that lined the gravel road running past our farm and collecting a variety of pets that included several cats, baby rabbits and even a goat that disappeared after one day.

My parents were religious, so, it was off to church twice every Sunday. I wasn't good at sitting still during church services: I remember receiving many pinches for wiggling and when I finally became bored with tormenting my sister I would drape my body across the laps of her and our mother because church time was also a great time to nap. After my accident, I would place my prosthetic in my mother's lap and whisper to her frantically that I had no pulse. Mom would struggle valiantly to contain her laughter and more often than not, would laugh silently with tears in her eyes.

School was a source of great fun for me as I had several favorite teachers and was a good student... for the most part! My memories of kindergarten boil down to my fellow female classmates and I flipping over on our mats at nap time to show what underwear we were wearing underneath our skirts. I was very jealous of the girls who were lucky enough to have underwear with the names of the week embroidered on them. My favorite companion was a female cousin who was just 4 months older than I and we were the best of friends who always ended up in the same classroom. By the time fifth grade rolled around, however, we were known as non-stop talkers and while punishments such as copying endless pages from the dictionary and writing sentences on the blackboard never stopped us, the patience of the school teachers did. Our chattering finally came to an end at the beginning of the fifth grade school year when we were put into separate classrooms. It would be high school before we shared a classroom again.

Life continued in the slow leisurely pace that was the 70s. Winters were long and brutally cold while summers were hot and steamy. Minnesota is known for its many lakes and we made good use of them. But in 1979, my dad decided to sell 200 of his 250 acres of farm land and buy a local grocery store in order to make a living. Commercial farming was starting to expand and my dad found it hard to make a profit off his 250 acres of land. I had just turned 12 in May that year and this was exciting news...I would finally be a "townie"...something some of us farm girls secretly coveted. I spent the first few months sweeping floors, shelving canned goods, candling eggs, bagging groceries, delivering groceries and helping customers at the deli counter with my favorite employee, Irene. At the tender age of 12, while I wasn't allowed to even consider having a boyfriend, I developed a major crush on Irene's youngest son, David who was a bit older than me. In my young star-crossed eyes he was the most beautiful person in the world: crystal blue eyes, long hair and he rode around town on a Harley. He was fully aware of my crush and while he didn't acknowledge it, he continued to treat me with a sweetness and gentleness that made me adore him even more. I wax poetic about this man and he will forever be a prince among men, because his act of incredible sensitivity on one of the darkest days of my life will never be forgotten. Each day at the grocery store was busy the summer of 1979 and I was a happy, healthy girl on the cusp of becoming a teenager. I was carefree with not a worry in the world.

Then came August when my life changed irrevocably. Life as I knew it would end and the little girl I had been would cease to exist.

AUGUST 15, 1979

August 15, 1979 started out the same as every other day. It was hot that summer, so I dressed in my favorite tank top, shorts and Keds and rode to work with my parents. I spent the day doing the tasks my mother assigned me. I remember wasting time in the cooler where we kept extra milk and eggs for stocking because it was so nice and cool and I wasn't in the mood to run errands outside in the humid air. The store wasn't huge, it was one of two in town and we were always busy. We had several employees – including my sister and brother when they were available. My sister had graduated from high school that year and had already moved to a larger town. My brother hated working in the store and at age 14 was off doing who knows what. My eldest brother, Mike, was married with a family of his own and lived in a town 30 miles away. I had just turned 13 in May, so, I had no other option but to go to work at the grocery store each day with my parents. I actually enjoyed working at the store most days, because, although I was still rather shy, being in the hustle and bustle atmosphere like the store's gave me the courage to come out of my shell and interact with the variety of customers that came in. I delivered groceries to the little old ladies and men in town who always invited me to stay and chat for a bit, providing delicious treats for me to enjoy; older folks seemed to be fascinated with the "little brown girl" at the corner grocery and I felt like a mini celebrity around them.

The store closed at 6 pm on most days and on this particular evening, several customers had stayed past closing time. It was still hot and humid outside and we were all ready to get home so that we could relax. My mother and father were at the front of the store closing out the cash registers and trying to shoo out the stragglers so they could lock the doors. I was sent to the meat room to start the clean-up process. The meat room was a small room at the back of the store that was filled with saws, grinders and extremely sharp knives. In those days, meat was rarely pre-packaged. My dad and Irene would cut meat to the customer's specifications and there were several sides of beef, bacon, pork and chicken carcasses hanging in a large metal freezer. Hamburger was freshly ground several times a day in a giant meat grinder and deli meats and cheeses were sliced from 5 lb blocks each day. My dad was meticulous when it came to his meat room and he demanded that everyone who worked in the room follow his rules by washing their hands frequently and keeping the large wooden block table, knives and machines sterilized with bleach and hot water. I never wanted to work in that room by choice because the machines were loud and intimidating, however, I preferred to while away the hours in the company of Irene over the other employees and there was nothing that could have prevented me from spending time with her – not even the scary meat room. Irene

Hofmann was German and spoke with an accent. She always told the best stories and jokes – and – she was David's mom. She adored me and treated me like the daughter she'd never had. I would spend hours gabbing with her and helping her as best I could in the meat room.

At 6:10 pm that evening, I was alone in the meat room, as most of the store employees had gone home for the day, trying to figure out where to begin clean up. On this particular night, trying to be helpful, I decided to tackle the biggest more complex machines first: the behemoth grinder being the most difficult and time-consuming machine to clean. It was a heavy, ugly machine that had several pieces that had to be removed so that they could be thoroughly cleaned. There was a broken part within the grinder that had to be manually pushed out and then the grinder restarted to complete the process of dismantling. I had watched the other store employees clean the grinder and felt I could safely clean it, as well. At 6:17 pm, I started to dismantle the heavy grinder and when it came time to give the broken part a push, I did so with my right hand (I was right-handed at the time) and kept my left hand on the start button because I knew I had just seconds to start the grinder to push the part out completely. For whatever reason – inexperience or a misjudgment of the timing, at 6: 18 pm, I turned the grinder on too quickly and the tips of the fingers of my right hand became trapped. I was able to shut the machine off within seconds. The pain was so intense – worse than anything else I had ever felt – that I began screaming hysterically – wanting only for someone to stop the excruciating pain. My mother, my wonderful, beautiful mother – upon hearing her youngest child screaming hysterically, ran from the front of the store to the back of the store into the meat room. My screams were coming non-stop and so loud; she thought the machine was still on. She pushed the switch back to the "on" position thinking she was stopping the machine and in an instant, my life changed forever. My forearm was pulled into the machine almost in the same instant when my mother realized her mistake. She flipped the switch back to "off". But it was too late. My arm has become hamburger inside the grinder. Both of us are momentarily stunned into silence and then the hell begins anew.

Cut to Scene 1:

My breathing is shallow and I feel faint. My entire body is slowly becoming numb from both pain and shock. My sense of hearing has become painfully acute and in my mind, my breathing sounds as loud as a freight train rushing through the room, but each breath seems to come as slow as molasses. Through the lethargy overtaking me, I feel the blood of my body draining out of me. I look at the three fingers poking out of the end of the machine, they are still intact, the nails still pink and I do not see blood which makes me wonder where all my blood is going to. My sense of reality is painfully honed in on what seems like the never ending screams and sobs coming out of the mouth of my mother. Somewhere in the fog of my brain, I hear someone hysterically begging rescue to come to Tensen's Grocery and that there has been a terrible accident. I am crouched in a painfully awkward position by now and my back is starting to cramp. Then there is the pain itself. The terrible, awful, nearly indescribable pain – so enormous and encompassing, that it transports me to another realm of consciousness. My young self cannot comprehend the level of pain that I am in. All I know is that I want it to go away so that I may sleep a painless sleep. My brain is telling me to close my eyes and go to sleep. I feel strangely pulled towards a quiet I have never felt before. Sleep. Sleep. Sleep. Time stands still. The frantic chaos that an emergency brings is happening all around me, yet I feel totally removed from it. I am rudely jolted by a loud noise and the first thought that enters my semi-conscious self is for my father.... I see him through a cut-out window between the meat room and the deli counter. He is pale, silent, with tears running down his face. I cannot see my mom, but I hear her. She has been crying hysterically the entire time and the child that I am begs her to help me. But, I do not seem to have the strength to open my mouth to say the words out loud. I am so very, very tired. It sounds as though there are several people sobbing, but I cannot see them and quite frankly, the sounds grated on my raw nerves. An endless loop of three sentences begins playing in my head. I am pleading to an audience that cannot hear me: "This hurts. Take it off, it hurts. It's so heavy it hurts, take it off." This loop swirls around my brain until it creates a storm of words that threatens to overtake my entire body. No one can hear me. I am alone in my head. I am so tired; I am going to close my eyes now. Good night, mom. Good night, dad.

Suddenly, the small room is filled with men dressed from head to toe in their fire and rescue gear. And I am jolted back to the present. These men are the fathers, grandfathers, uncles and brothers of my classmates. Each and every one of them has tears glistening in their eyes and some hastily try to wipe away the tears rolling down their strong, tanned faces. At some point, my best friend's dad, Ed, sits on the floor behind me, gingerly lifts me on to his lap and carefully cradles me so that I can get relief from my cramped posture. His right arm curves around my thin body; with his right hand holding the weight of my trapped arm and with his left hand, he feeds me M&M's in an effort to keep me awake. I still cannot see my mom and dad, but hear my mother: still sobbing somewhere outside of the room. A disembodied voice says: "keep mom and dad out of the room". A different voice speaks directly to me, calling my name and whoever it is, tells me that I must stay awake and I must remain strong. I am told that I must not cry because my mother is upset and I cannot let her see me crying.

Dear god in heaven....without warning, it's as if the mother of all chainsaws is ripping through my right arm: someone is trying to twist the bell of the grinder off the machine. I hear myself screaming hysterically again, the pain is so intense that the screams coming out of my mouth are beyond anything comprehensible. It takes what seems like an excruciating lifetime before several members of the rescue squad are finally successful in separating the bell from the rest of the machine. My arm is still one with the grinder, because they cannot remove it without me dying from blood loss and shock. The bell will travel with me to the emergency room.

There is now a new problem: space is tight in this room. I am a little girl attached to a large metal bell and they must find a way to lift me over the meat display counter in order to get me to the ambulance that is waiting by the side door. Two men gently lift me over the counter into the arms of two firemen standing on the other side of the case. As I am being lifted, my eyes are drawn to the front of the store which has two large plate glass windows that face the main street. The scene that meets my eyes is simply amazing. There is a huge crowd of people – hundreds it seems – standing in the streets. People pressed against the glass windows and I can see one person very clearly through the never ending haze of pain. He is a classmate of mine named Michael. He is already one of the most popular male athletes my age and certainly one of the cutest. He is wearing a red shirt with the Coca-Cola emblem emblazoned in white on the front and he is the only bright color I see as I hazily wonder through the fog of my brain why so many people are standing in the streets outside the grocery store.

I am carried in someone's arms through the side door which is on the south side of the building. There are so many people lining the street that I cannot see the large bank building that sits across the street from our grocery store. There is a crowd of what seems to be hundreds of men, women and children and they are all eerily silent. The only sounds I hear are the sirens blaring from the many rescue vehicles parked every which way around the store. An ambulance is parked directly in front of the side door and police cars in front of it waiting to escort me to the nearest hospital which is 30 miles away in a town called Willmar. My vision clears a little and I see Him. It is David and he is sitting on one of his Harley Davidson motorcycles that he's parked directly behind the ambulance. He looks directly into my eyes and gives me a sweet, gentle smile and I stick my tongue out at him.

I am carefully bundled into the back of the ambulance as though I am made of the most fragile glass and placed tenderly into the waiting arms of a doctor and an ambulance attendant. My mother sits up front, sandwiched between the driver and another ambulance attendant. I can hear her from the back, she is still crying softly. The doors close and we are off in a blare of sirens and whirling lights with our police escort. I hear the driver talking into his mic – something about our estimated time of arrival. There will be a police escort from the Willmar police department who will meet the ambulance at the halfway point and escort it, lights and sirens, to the hospital. Although I am exhausted and just want to go to sleep, I begin to feel strangely at peace, as though once again, I am far removed from the activity around me. The doctor gently interrupts my slumber repeatedly: "Wake up, Lorie – you can't go to sleep, Honey. Wake up". But, I no longer feel anything. I am weightless. There is no more pain. I vaguely hear the doctor say something but his voice is coming from a tunnel. Suddenly, the ambulance attendant who is in the back with me begins speaking frantically into his mic: "We are losing her, HURRY... We're gonna lose her! DO NOT tell the mother! DO NOT tell the mother!! HURRY, we're losing her!!" Through the numbness taking over my body, I briefly wonder, yet again, who this person is talking about and then, thankfully, there are no more sounds at all.

Lorie Tensen

LITTLE-GIRL LOST

Did I die at that moment? I do not know and cannot say for sure. There is something to be said about the absence of sound, smell, sight and sensation that is unconsciousness. Even so, decades later, I am nearly overcome with a rush of memories when I think back on the events of that day. While there were many blessed moments of oblivion during the seemingly endless hours of that evening, there were even more moments of sheer agony. I tend to remember that day in the third person as a sort of emotional defense mechanism. What happened to me was so physically and mentally excruciating, that remembering – let alone discussing – that day as me, first person, still brings tears to my eyes and my missing limb contracts in the pain of remembrance. As an adult, I can hardly bear to imagine having to go through such a painful accident such as that. The child in me is grateful that what I put to pen and paper at this moment are memories. So, let us now return to August 15, 1979.

When I regain consciousness, it is to the soothing sounds of a man's voice gently calling my name. I open my eyes to bright lights and a blur of human figures and a flurry of activity in my periphery vision. I roll my eyes to the left and see a handsome young man in hospital scrubs. He's holding a pair of scissors and says: "Honey, I need to cut your shirt off." I am mortified. I am barely 13 and I am wearing a training bra. I start to cry and mumble "no, it's my favorite shirt" over and over again. As he gently cuts through the straps of my shirt and bra, he quietly says again: "it's okay, sweetie, I'll be careful, it's okay, please don't cry". His words are the last thing I remember when yet again, the blessed relief of unconsciousness over takes me.

The next time I open my eyes, it is because I have woken myself up with my own screams. I have come out of anesthesia too quickly and am screaming for my mother. I can focus on nothing but the fact that I want my mom. Within moments, there is a nurse at my side. She is very gentle as she strokes my arm and speaks in a calm and quiet tone. She says: "Hi, Honey. You are in the ICU recovery room and your mom and dad are just outside the door." I do not understand what she is saying and I don't care. I cry myself back into unconsciousness. There are no more memories from this moment in the ICU recovery room until I wake up in a private room surrounded by members of my family. I am 13 years old and my life has been changed forever.

It is a bewilderingly and busy time. I am weak from blood loss and near death. I want to hide in the bosom of my family because I am emotionally shattered and frightened. I have had my right arm amputated just inches below the elbow and underneath the thick bandages, my stump is raw and sore. I cannot even begin to comprehend the scope of how this accident will alter my life and I am not ready to think about it. I am in an incredible amount of pain, but I do not cry. I know that while I am physically present, the personality and spirit and innocence of the girl I used to be is gone. I have no clue how I should be reacting physically, mentally and emotionally, so, I withdraw into my own little world. I have the strange sensation that something within me has died, yet I cannot find the words to accurately describe to my family the dramatic change that has occurred not only to my physical self, but to my mental and emotional self, as well. From the moment I am moved out of the ICU recovery room, I can recall doctors and nurses telling me just how strong and brave I was and that despite the trauma I've been through, they are amazed at my stoicism and lack of tears. I hear nurses conversing at the nurses' station located just outside my door and my name comes up quite frequently in their conversations. "She's such a brave little girl. She didn't cry once!"

I do not want to upset my family by telling them just how very scared I really am, so, I say nothing. In the world outside of my private room within Rice Memorial Hospital, I have become a bit of a minor (very minor) celebrity – albeit a reluctant one who had never intended on being in the spotlight. Each day I received at least one giant bag of mail from the post office filled to near bursting. Most days, there were two of these large bags. They contain beautifully wrapped packages containing stuffed animals, candy, chocolates and toys. The hundreds of cards contain money and prayer tokens. My family and the nurses are kept busy taping cards to the walls of my hospital room and within days, we cannot see the paint color on the walls because the countless cards have become colorful wallpaper. The majority of names signed at the bottoms of these cards are those of strangers – people who have heard the story from prayer chains across the country, friends of friends and in some places, newspapers and radio. They have generously showed their support for me and my situation by sending gifts. My mother tells me that news of my accident has become national: strangers have heard about the little girl who lost her arm in a "freak" accident in states as far away from Minnesota as New Mexico and Florida. Flower and balloon bouquets arrive daily in mass proportions.

My family brings home numerous bouquets of flowers each day and gives every nurse's station a fresh vase of flowers on an almost daily basis. Visitors appear each day, arriving at all hours from morning until late at night – even during my meal and rest times and make their way to the hospital floor where my room is located. The hospital finally decides to limit my visitors to a certain number each day because there are simply too many of them and so many of them are complete strangers. The list is ultimately narrowed down to close family and friends. I find out later that several friends of my sister were turned away. After just a day in the hospital, I only wanted my family around me because I was mentally exhausted by all of the crying that occurs when people visit and quite frankly, I have yet to process the enormity of what has happened to me. Often times, the allowed visits quickly become too overwhelming. I try to curl up in my hospital bed quietly, my body and soul numbed by pain medication and sheer exhaustion but, the visitors stay in my room and stand in a corner with my parents, chatting endlessly, as though they are at a social gathering and I am a mouse in the corner. I remember pushing my body and heavily bandaged arm as deeply into the mattress as possible when they looked directly at me because the pity in their eyes was almost too much to bear. I am too wrapped up within my own pain and misery and too naive to appreciate the fact that these kind visitors were trying to offer comfort to my family and I by visiting and being social.

There was no time set aside for me to grieve my loss or show any sign of weakness. I was told over and over on a daily basis by nearly everyone that I must swallow my own fears, "pray to the Lord for strength and guidance", and act as a source of comfort and strength for my family because they would gain courage through my resilience. Someone bluntly tells me that shedding tears won't make my arm grow back and that I must move forward so as to begin the healing process. I bristle in anger when I recall some of the advice that was given to me at a time when I was so fragile. I was so scared that if I showed any sign of weakness, my family would fall apart. I did not tell my mother about the unwanted advice until I wrote this book. It was a heavy burden I bore for many years.

While it might seem strange to some, all things considered, there was never any resentment or anger towards my parents for not insulating me from the outside world during this difficult time. From conversations with my mother during the writing of this book, I knew that at the time, both my mother and father were suffering from an extreme sense of guilt and helplessness and were struggling find ways to help their daughter navigate the rocky road that lay ahead of her. They were offered no counseling or resources from the hospital and did the best that they could in light of the situation. My family tried their best not to treat me any differently than they had before, but on hindsight, I can vividly recall the naked grief in my parents eyes, the numerous conversations I overheard taking place outside the door of my hospital room between my parents, visitors and hospital personnel with my mother and father's voices raw with pain and the helplessness in the eyes of my siblings when they came to visit despite the jokes they told in an attempt to make me smile each day. My mother always seemed to be on the verge of tears and even then, I could sense that it was a struggle for her to keep them at bay when she was with me. My father was stoic, but there was a haunted look deep within his eyes whenever he was around me that lasted until the day he died.

After the numerous comments made by well-meaning people, I felt an incredible amount of responsibility for my entire family's emotional well-being and so much so that I forced myself to be silent and strong and continued to keep my tears and fears to myself. I made up my mind to do whatever it took to get back to "normal". One of my favorite days was the day my wonderful sister stopped by my hospital room with a large artist pad, pencils and pens so that I could learn how to write with my left hand. Each day, I forced myself to practice writing for hours, painstakingly printing my name and the letters of the alphabet over and over again with my poor overworked left hand. Sometimes, I would get frustrated at the seemingly slow progress I made, and tears would stain the paper, but I was stubborn. I persevered and within two weeks, I was writing fairly legibly with my left hand. When I knew I would be left alone for a while, I practiced tying my tennis shoes with my teeth (which is incredibly difficult), buttoning buttons and zipping zippers with one hand and despite the clumsiness of those tasks, I was able to dress myself in something other than pajamas by the time I left the hospital.

Although I was being treated like a princess and embarrassingly indulged and pampered by the nursing staff, I was overwhelmed with the attention, homesick, and still in a lot of pain. My arm was heavily bandaged and during bandage changes and inspections, I forced myself to stare at the short tender stump that had not become what is left of my right arm. A doctor patiently showed me how to wash my tender stump in Dreft baby laundry soap and how to gently pat it dry without inadvertently pulling out the many stitches. I remember having to bite my lip in a rush of emotions each time, but I refused to cry. I endured endless visits from doctors who probe my tender flesh and asked questions until I want to scream. My parents and I are informed that once my stitches are removed and there is more healing, I will be fitted for a prosthetic with a hook first and once I learn how to manipulate that I will be measured again for what is called a myo-electric or cosmetic prosthesis that will eventually act as the permanent replacement for the limb that was severed in the accident. Privately, I am sickened because I feel so ugly and damaged. I try not to vomit when I see what prosthetic limbs look like and I begin to get headaches whenever the discussion turns to that subject. I look into my parent's eyes as they discuss, in falsely cheerful voices, how exciting it will be for me when I get my fake arm. I scream how much I hate my life into my pillow when they go home each night but, I do not cry or complain in their presence. Ten days after my accident, I am released from the hospital.

STARTING OVER: AGAIN AND AGAIN AND AGAIN

It is now close to the end of August, school will start after Labor Day because this is a farming community and this will be my first year in the building that houses both the middle school and high school. I have been looking forward to being an official 7th grader but this year I will not be starting school with my classmates. Instead, I will spend the remainder of August and the first few weeks of September with a "minder". I am still incredibly weak and unsteady and cannot be left alone. My right limb is still heavily wrapped and tender and it would be quite painful if I were jostled by accident in the busy hallways that are filled with students during class changes. I will spend the majority of each day with friends of our family, the Swanson's, until significantly more healing has taken place and I am physically able to endure a long school day.

I soon find myself bored beyond belief, and while I do not intend to come across as ungracious, I am exhausted with the hours spent opening the non-stop cards and gifts that continue to pour in. My unseasoned left hand continually cramps from the laborious attempts to hand write legible thank you notes and there are days when I can barely open and close it. At some point, my left hand becomes too sore to finish writing the scores of "thank you" notes that remain, so, my parents submit a "thank you column" from my family to the general public in several local newspapers. Even at the age of 13, I was overwhelmed by the indescribable love and support the community of Brooten, as well as, the folks from numerous towns; cities and states were giving to me. I did not feel that I deserved special attention, but know that it was the strength, support and love of these people that provided the foundation for getting through those difficult weeks following my accident.

One might assume that a child having suffered such a traumatic experience would have been treated with kid gloves and babied by family and friends. It is to my benefit that my family did not give me any slack. I was, of course, given time to heal physically...but that was it. My parents are both products of hearty Dutch farmer stock and that apparently rubbed off on me. Much to the surprise of everyone but my immediate family, I started school in September. I did not want to fall too far behind in my classes and missed my friends. So, with my tender right arm in a sling (no prosthetic, yet), I started 7th grade. My classmates made my first few months bearable: my books were carried, my shoes tied for me and I was excused from anything that required physical exertion. I spent several weeks attending school only half days until I could last a full day without needing to rest. Mentally and emotionally, however, I was still numb to the core.

For my peers, life seemed to continue as though everything was fine, but it wasn't fine for me. I did not have a counselor, psychologist, or psychiatrist made available to me so that I could have a safe, neutral outlet for all the emotions and fears that I was holding inside. I was a kid – and despite having returned to life as a middle school student, my life had changed irrevocably and I had no clue how to properly adjust to the changes. No one in my life had the foresight to give me instruction and guidance on how to function as an amputee. Here I was, a 13-year old girl: a time when kids that age are starting to think about the opposite sex and experiencing changes in their bodies.

I was damaged physically, mentally and emotionally with no one to talk to. I was lost – adrift in a sea of a very frightening unknown. I began to remove myself from the reality of the outside world, after all, I was so ugly now, and no one would want to be seen with me after the novelty wore off – let alone – date me when I turned 16! So, beginning in the fall of 1979, my physical self- remained present, but the innocent Lorie that existed before August 15, was ruthlessly stamped into the furthest recesses of my mind. The "new" Lorie was indestructible: nothing and no one could pierce through the walls I built around myself. Regrets and tears were not allowed because I knew that if I gave in to those emotions, I would drown in a sea of self-pity, sorrow and fear. I developed an outgoing persona that I became known for and forced myself out of my shy shell by becoming the "funny girl" in class. I joked with teachers, tried to make friends with everyone, practiced my flirting skills on as many boys as possible, yet rarely allowed anyone to get close to the real me. I knew I was lying to myself and everyone around me. But this false bravado became my only source of survival.

Meanwhile, outside of school, there were numerous trips each year to an occupational therapist in Willmar, Minnesota and Gillette Children's Specialty Care in St. Paul, Minnesota which was an exhausting 6 hour round trip from my home town. Let us begin with the occupational therapist: my therapist was a woman who unwittingly did more damage to my self-esteem than any other one person during the first 3-months following my accident. While I can be fairly certain that she did not purposely intend to harm me, her approach to therapy cemented the last brick in the wall of the emotional armor I had been building to protect my tender feelings from hurtful words, looks and my own angst.

She and I met once a week for several weeks, and in her defense, while she wasn't a first year therapist by any means, I was her first biracial patient and her first child amputee patient. She was uncomfortable around me and I knew it. She hesitated to touch me and instead of approaching me with the kindness, warmth and gentleness needed in a situation with a child who is still reeling from a life-changing event, she dealt with me in a brisk, cold, impersonal manner and I could not wait for my sessions with her to end. There were never any discussions with either my mother, who accompanied me to these appointments, or me regarding how to transition back to real life after a lengthy absence. There was never any discussion on how to field questions or how my parents could prepare the school personnel on how to assist my transition back as a student. As a child, I already had a near crippling fear of being stared at and touched by strangers fascinated with my skin color. I was now nearly catatonic at times, not wanting to go to towns outside of Brooten – especially wearing short sleeved shirts. I had irrationally convinced myself that not only would people stare because I had brown skin; they would now be staring and pointing at me because I wore a metal hook on my right arm. Not once did the therapist address my fears. Did I express those fears? No, I was a 13-year old girl in a room with a professional therapist. Occupational and Physical Therapists today are trained to look for every possible scenario that could hinder a patient's recovery. In 1979, I'll have to assume this was not the case. My mother, having been raised not to question "experts", told me years later that while she had not liked my occupational therapist from the very beginning, she had not felt it was her place to question the woman's tactics until it was too late.

When I was still a patient at Rice Memorial Hospital in Willmar after my accident, I was told that in order to be fitted with a cosmetic prosthetic that was much more aesthetically pleasing in that: a) it would be covered with a skin that would come close to matching my own skin color, b) it would be designed to match the length and width of my natural arm and, c) it would operate with the use of electrodes pressed against my muscles and a battery, I first needed to learn how to control my arm and shoulder muscles by using an unwieldy prosthetic with a metal hook at the end. The prosthetic was just plain ugly. No exaggeration and no other words to describe it. It was fashioned out of a pale unnatural looking pink plastic and was basically a shell 14 inches long with a metal hook at the end.

An uncomfortable, hard plastic strap wrapped around my left shoulder and I learned how to control the opening and closing of the hook by tightening my left shoulder muscles and pushing against the strap and my right shoulder muscles to push down into the prosthetic. These opposing forces caused the hook to open and also, with daily use, rebuilt the muscle tone I had lost. It was a process I had to think about each time I did it, after all, each day we open and close our hands and move the rest of our body about without giving it a second thought. I had to learn how to compensate for the loss of my limb and I had to learn how to use what used to be my dominant hand in a new way. Patience was not my strong-suit and I was easily frustrated with the assignments I was given. For example: I would have to build a tower out of small blocks. It was an excruciatingly slow and somewhat painful process to manipulate my shoulders so that I could pick up a small block with the hook and place it on another. I would be mentally and physically exhausted by hour's end. Encouragement consisted of: "You need to learn this or you'll have to wear a hook forever." This was negative reinforcement that actually worked because she knew I hated the hook and refused to wear it at home or in public.

The toughest assignment I was given petrified me: the occupational therapist told me I had to walk around Willmar (a town of several thousand at that time – much larger than Brooten and unfamiliar to me) dressed in short sleeved shirts wearing the metal hook. Session after session, I stubbornly wore a sweatshirt and stuck the hook into the sweatshirt pocket or my right pants pocket and refused to take it out as I walked through the streets of Willmar. I would stare straight ahead as I walked and looked neither left nor right or directly into anyone's face. The therapist and my mother would trail several steps behind me and my mother was told she could not walk beside me. Mom told me many years later that every time we went out on those walkabouts she would follow me with angry tears in her eyes, knowing how difficult the assignment was for me. She said she had felt such anger with the occupational therapist for pushing me to do something I was not mentally or emotionally ready for and in a manner that seemed callous. The therapist would at times cajole and threaten me as she tried to convince me to remove the hook from my pocket. Finally, frustrated with my stubbornness, the therapist sat me down and bluntly told me that she would not give approval for me to be fitted for the more human looking prosthetic until I successfully completed a walk around town in a short sleeved shirt, with both arms hanging at my sides. I was devastated: I already felt so ugly and in my naive mind, wearing a cosmetic prosthetic would be less noticeable than the metal hook. Adolescents have no desire to stand out in a crowd and I was especially sensitive. My parents left the choice up to me. I could wear the hook for as long as it took, or, remove my sweatshirt at the next therapy session and take my hand out of my pocket.

On the second to last session, I did it. I remember telling both my mother and the therapist determinedly that I was going to do this by myself. They were not to come near me on this walk and they were not to talk to me at all. I took a deep breath, removed my favorite sweatshirt and walked out the door. We spent the entire hour outside walking around downtown Willmar stopping at several stores along the way. I didn't try to hide my right arm in any way, but kept both arms hanging by my side. There was a rush of emotions: sadness, fear, humiliation, joy and excitement. I had done the impossible: I had taken my hand out of my pocket! I felt triumph that I had overcome my fear, anger that I had been forced to do complete this assignment and a keen sense of loss: yet again, my innocence had been stripped from me...I felt the entire town had just seen me naked.

At the final occupational therapy session, we had a celebration: my mother surprised me with a chocolate cake – my favorite – baked in the shape of an arm and an empty pocket that sat to the side. For the first time in months, the therapist relaxed with me and we shared several laughs over her inability to conquer my stubbornness. She said I had been the toughest patient she had ever worked with...which gave me much satisfaction! This was a pivotal moment in my life and really, it was a pivotal moment in the lives of my mother and father. It was my acknowledgment, albeit a reluctantly given acknowledgment, that a prosthetic limb would forever be a part of my body. I could no longer hide behind my sling or the comfort of familiar surroundings and a community that was used to seeing me hide my stump in a sling, which I had thought, made the loss of limb less noticeable.

No one in my home town pointed a finger at me or made me feel "less than". Hundreds of people in Brooten knew about my accident and had blessedly provided the safety of a comfort zone around me that I never wanted to leave. However, because I had not received any psychological counseling that would have guided me through the grief and sense of loss I'd experienced, as well as, prepared me for what was to come, I existed in a sort of twilight zone of my own design: obviously missing a limb, but pretending nothing was amiss.

In an extremely messed up way, I had convinced myself that if I hid what was missing and didn't look down, I could pretend I was still whole. I could pretend that tying my shoes with my teeth was a neat party trick and that wearing clothes without buttons and zippers made getting ready much quicker and that cutting my hair short was so my mother would no longer be burdened with braiding my hair. Wearing a prosthetic was an in-your-face-this-is-fake reality to me. I'd gone out in public wearing a hook; I would soon be fitted with a cosmetic prosthesis and somehow knew I would no longer be allowed to hide in my make-believe world anymore. I would, yet again, become a topic of conversation and of course, I imagined years of never-ending curiosity from lookie-lou's and dreaded the many upcoming conversations and questions that would arise with this new gadget poking out of my sleeve and I just knew there would be tons of questions I would have to answer and I would be expected to politely answer them all: how did it work, did it hurt to wear, how did it stay on my stump and what did that stump look like, by the way? So my reality became plastic, or rather, my plastic became reality. This new-found reality check also brought several emotionally painful truths that I had not wanted to face: never again would I be able to do simple things with my right and left hands that I had taken for granted for the first 12 years of my life: steeple all 10 finger tips, interlace my fingers, feel the sting of a burn or the softness of human touch stroking my right arm and hand. I remember the sensations in my fingers and hands when I used to play my favorite church game...did you play this one, too? I would interlace my fingers and chant: "here is the church, here is the steeple, open the doors and see all the people"....wiggling my fingers and thumbs.....I cry.

The numerous trips to Gillette Children's Specialty Care Hospital in St. Paul, Minnesota were also emotionally and physically exhausting and yet, I truly enjoyed the time

I got to spend with my mom and dad. My dad hated driving in big cities and it took several trips before we succeeded in arriving at the hospital doors without an unplanned trip through a suburb of the Twin Cities! My parents weren't the type to spoil their children but, knowing how emotionally and physically exhausted I would be by day's end, they would pack my favorite foods for the ride to the hospital and stop at every Dairy Queen for a Peanut Buster Parfait on the trip home. Yes, we stopped at every Dairy Queen and yes, I was a chunky eighth grader...don't judge!

Because we lived three hours away from the Twin Cities, the day would start at 3 am in order to make sure we made it on time to my first appointment which started at 7 am. I would curl up in the back seat of the car with a blanket and pillow and sleep until we reached Golden Valley. My day was scheduled minute by minute and packed with non-stop appointments from 7 am to 5 pm. My parents were allowed to sit in on a couple of the appointments, but most of the day I was on my own, accompanied by a hospital minder. I would meet with physical therapists, occupational therapists, hospital psychologists, psychiatrists, and prosthetist technicians, groups of residents, physicians and surgeons. I was poked, prodded, asked endless questions and then poked and prodded some more. By the end of the day, when I was cranky, tired and missing my parents, I had my least favorite appointment: I was brought into a large room without my parents, filled to standing room only, with 50 or more people. Most of them were folks I'd had appointments with throughout the day along but there were also several unfamiliar faces: interns, residents, nurses and hospital personnel from other areas of the hospital who were there to observe. Because I had had my arm amputated as an adolescent in a traumatic accident, my case was considered unique and I was a case study for the hospital until I turned eighteen. I would sit in a chair that had been placed in the center of the room and the question-and-answer session of my day would begin. At times, I would be asked several questions directly, but for the most part, the various groups I'd had appointments with would be quizzed for an hour or two and I would sit quietly and listen. It was very uncomfortable and I would breathe a sigh of relief as soon as I was allowed out of the hot seat and escorted back to my parents.

There were also occasions where I had to stay overnight at the hospital and those occasions was fun: Gillette Children's Specialty Hospital is an amazing facility that specializes in the diagnosis and treatment of children, teenagers and adults who have disabilities and complex medical conditions. An overnight at the hospital was like a fun-sleepover camp. Meals would consist of all the junk food my parents didn't allow at home and we would be allowed to race through the hallways and play games on the kids ward. I was always able to forget my own disability and raw feelings when I played with tiny babies in the waiting room and read stories to the toddlers. The majorities of these children were born with congenital defects and were missing both arms and legs. They were at the hospital to be fitted with the tiniest prosthetic limbs and I was ashamed that I was so emotionally weak while they greeted the world with big bright smiles. These beautiful children seemed to be otherwise untouched by their various disabilities and to those little boys and girls I was just a fun, big kid who loved to play with them and read stories to them. Those were the moments when I felt like nothing was amiss.

After a couple of years, I had graduated to a point where I began to spend less time at Gillette – maybe once a year - and instead, had several appointments each year at Otto Bock in Golden Valley. Otto Bock is a German prosthetics company that was fairly new at the time and I was one of their newest and youngest upper extremity clients. My favorite technician was Larry Mott and he and I became fast friends. Otto Bock was in the process of designing new and innovative prosthetics for both upper and lower extremities. Engineers from Germany and

Japan would meet in locked down workshops at Otto Bock and every once in a while, I was able to convince Larry to sneak me in. What I saw in the 1970s and early 1980s became the foundation for the prosthetics we see today. Simply amazing and a fascinatingly sci-fi world: robotic arms and legs would be spinning slowly on pedestals. Engineers would use computers to open and close hands and simulate wrist turning. Robotic feet would mimic walking and running motions in a macabre dance on the middle of a table. I felt as though I'd been let in on a great secret and looked forward to my Otto Bock days.

While I did not particularly like having a right arm that was plastic, I felt naked without it. I quickly learned how to use my myo-electric prosthetic arm and was able to do simple tasks like tying my shoes and grasping objects such as door handles. Without it, my right sleeve hung empty and I felt handicapped and conspicuous. And while I knew that I could function 10 times better with my prosthetic than without it, I was still extremely hard on myself when it came to my physical appearance. In my eyes, I was ugly. My skin was brown. I was starting to get chunky and I had a fake arm. I became an expert at avoiding direct looks at my prosthetic in the mirror. My friends and family would probably say they saw nothing amiss, but inside, I was an ever roiling mass of mixed emotions. I felt like a pot of water that was about to boil over and I was struggling to keep my emotions under control. When I entered high school, I just wanted to fit in and be a normal teenager. But "normal" to me seemed so different than the "normal" of my best girlfriends. I wasn't normal – I was damaged goods and I could not psychologically get beyond that. Today, it's so difficult to explain the tug-of-war in my mind during my teenage years. As an adult, having read countless stories about amputees who've lost limbs in wars and accidents and accepted their new normal with ease, I wonder at my own fragility and the length of time it took for me to find my way. But, I digress. On the one hand, I was an honor roll student, active in many extracurricular activities, continued to play piano, sing and was well-liked by my peers, teachers and community. I liked the outgoing Lorie, but she was a newer personality on the scene and I did not have enough confidence in myself to trust that this personality was real. On the other, there was the continued dark presence of low self-esteem and self-doubt that I could not conquer. I did not feel sorry for myself. I did not wish for my life to go back to the way it had been before my accident. But, there was tentativeness behind every action I took and I was always prepared for rejection and inevitably surprised by acceptance. I never trusted the acceptance that was so often readily given and I continually imagined that I was being pitied behind my back. For example: I wanted desperately to be nominated as a candidate for Princess or Queen of the Homecoming and Sno Daze courts, but I was too timid to voice my desires out loud. I was so afraid people would vote for me because they felt sorry for the one-armed girl and I refused to be pitied. So I became the entertainment, instead. I hosted the programs, sang songs, told jokes, and presented the royal courts. I threw myself into the hosting duties and stoically pretended that I was where I wanted to be. I look back today and while I feel sorry for the girl who struggled with this inner battle on a daily basis, I am amazed that I was able to hide my struggles from everyone and saddened that I felt so conflicted. It shouldn't have been that difficult for so many years. I knew I needed help that my family couldn't provide and I remember feeling lost and alone – I would lie in my bed at night and all I could think was that I was slowly drowning. I didn't know how to ask for help and who I would have asked had I known.

Throughout middle and high school, outside of the special treatment on the trips to Gillette, my family acted as though nothing had happened to me. Teachers, friends and family members were also advised to treat me like they would any other student with no special concessions or class requirements. I cannot remember a single time that we sat down and talked about my accident as a family. It was surreal and at times confusing, frustrating, and devastatingly difficult for me and so I decided I would never ask anyone, especially my family, for help of any kind or show my true emotions. I would carry on just like everyone else and pretend nothing had ever happened to me. Just months after my accident, I was sent back to work in the grocery store. It was not a place I had ever wanted to step foot in again. My parents, with good intentions, probably felt that this was a situation similar to falling off a horse....you don't stop riding forever, you dust yourself off and get right back on the horse. So, I dusted myself off and went back to work at the grocery story, but believe me: I was not about to march into that meat room and clean the meat grinder! I would hear the grinder running and as often as I could, escape outside or seal myself in the cooler so that I could no longer hear the grinding sound. The nightmares became day-mares whenever I worked at the store — which was every day - and it was a struggle to keep from dissolving in tears and hyperventilating in front of customers.

In school, I was not allowed to sit on the sidelines for any class. I participated in the wood shop class (saws, blades, noises that made me cringe), basketball, volleyball, softball for physical education class and even typing classes. I was especially proud of myself when I received a B+ on my final typing exam. It was a major accomplishment for me because I had taken the same timed typing test that my classmates had taken and I could type 40 words a minute with one hand.

My low self-esteem and terrible body image manifested itself in what became a decade's long struggle with anorexia and bulimia. I began this journey as a sophomore in high school and at my lowest point found that my 5'9" frame was carrying just 109 pounds. I lived on corn bread and JELL-O for months at a time and surreptitiously smoked cigarettes in the bathroom of the grocery store or stuck my finger down my throat to maintain the weight. I wore sweatshirts in the summer and piled on heavy clothing during the harsh Minnesota winters to hide my skinny body from my parents.

My inner struggle overwhelmed me more often than not and there were times when I simply could not emotionally take it another minute. At the age of 16 just weeks before the end of the school year, I ran away from home. I wasn't planning on going far – just to the home of my former sister-in-law who lived in Willmar. After a tearful meeting with my parents, it was decided that I would go back home with them until exams were finished and then I would spend the entire summer with my sister-in-law and nieces. It was a much needed time-out that helped break the cycle of self-harm for a few months.

Another example of my extremely low self-esteem was how I dealt with my hair: from the day I was allowed to manage my own hair in the 7th grade, I began to cut it shorter and shorter eventually shaving it to the skull as an adult. Subconsciously, as with the anorexia and bulimia, I wanted to disappear. I am certain that my parents felt an incredible sense of helplessness: here was this child of theirs that they loved so much, who they knew was hurting beyond words and there was nothing they felt they could do that would help ease the pain. I rejected their way of showing me love often. Not because I was a spoiled brat of a kid, but because it wasn't enough. I was a very confused young lady who desperately needed counseling. I needed someone to give me permission to release my pent up emotions. Someone who would tell me that it was okay to cry, to grieve the loss of my limb and to say that it sucked that I had to experience this trauma and that I could and would survive intact. That someone never materialized and I continued to lose myself in non-stop activity playing the loud and boisterous class clown who volunteered for everything imaginable in an effort to mask my inner melt-down: a church missionary excursion the summer before my senior year of high school, President of my church youth group, co-editor of the 1984 year book, prom co-committee chairperson, senior class vice president, speech and drama teams, cheer leading squad and manager of the varsity volley ball team. I passed my driver's training exam and happily took advantage of having a license and access to a sporty mustang and without much studying, landed on the honor roll every semester.

I knew that I would never find my path in life if I stayed anywhere near the epicenter of my angst and so by the time I was a junior in high school, my mind was made up to leave small-town Brooten, Minnesota by any means necessary. I felt it was crucial to my sanity and so, when I graduated from high school, I moved to Grand Rapids, Michigan to attend a private Christian college.

OUT OF THE FRYING PAN....

Free at last, free at last — finally: freedom! I was hundreds of miles away from the watchful eyes of my parents and no one in the city of Grand Rapids knew anything about me or my accident aside from a couple of cousins who lived there, as well. There were black, white, brown and yellow people who called this city home, so, I felt confident that no one would take a second look at me. Unfortunately, this was not to be the case. It seemed many of my demons had followed me to college and I picked up a few more along the way. It was in Grand Rapids that I first heard the word "nigger" screamed at me when I was walking down the street. Unbeknownst to me, the school I would be attending was not known for its racial harmony. It was by no means segregated, but the whites stuck with whites, the very small group of black American students stuck with other black American students, the African students had their own social groups and the Asians and Canadians stayed quietly in the background. There were a few of us who were products of trans-racial adoption: we were the brown and yellow students who had been adopted into white, Christian Reformed families — families similar in all ways to the majority population of the white students that attended the school. I found that the white students readily accepted me and I made many new friends. However, several black American female students bluntly informed me that I was too different from them: my lighter toned skin, the cadence of my speech, the food I preferred, and the young white men I preferred to date. After just months at the school, I began receiving anonymous calls at night. Voices whispered through the phone that I was a snobby bitch who needed to go back to where I came from. But I recognized those voices and knew the names of the girls behind the calls. The calls and harassment occurred so frequently that by the end of my first semester I had made multiple trips to the Dean of Students for relief. I did not share this torment with my family during my phone calls home, because I was so afraid my parents would pressure me to return back to the safety of my home town. I was determined to stick it out and earn my degree.

I had an energetic roommate and fun-loving suite-mates my freshman year and found myself really enjoying dorm life. Over time, I developed a core group of wonderful friends who were from all different backgrounds and am still in touch with some of those ladies today. I cringe when I think of the many times I tried too hard to be accepted by flashing cash from an insurance settlement that was supposed to cover my living expenses. I bought my roommates lavish floral bouquets for their birthdays and sprang for pizza on several occasions before I figured out I wasn't getting anything in return. My academic life, unfortunately, really suffered. I had easily coasted through high school without really ever studying. While I wasn't a straight-A student, my report card usually listed only one or two B's and I was an honor-roll student. I assumed college would be just as easy for me. Au contraire – I found myself on academic probation in no time and had to take a class that was supposed to teach me how to study. I was lucky to pass my freshman year in college with a GPA that hovered just above failing. I did make an effort after that but, it wasn't anything to write home about. There was fun to be had, parties to attend and my very first boyfriend.

At college, people kept telling me I was "exotic" looking because I was neither black nor white. I was tall, thin and saucy in public, but shy in person. I'd had crushes in high school and had received a kiss or two, but my dad was extremely strict and scared the bejesus out of any young man who dared to look twice at me. I would argue until I cried and by the time he relented and gave his permission for a young man to date me, the young man would have turned tail and run. It was too much effort to date Gerard Tensen's youngest daughter. Dear Reader: please remember that I had considered myself physically ugly since my accident at the tender age of 13. I believed with all my heart that I would never meet anyone who would look beyond the prosthetic limb and not only accept me for me, but who actually would want to be seen in public with me. Would any young man really want to be known as the guy with the-one armed girlfriend and get made fun of by his buddies? In my mind, this was a very real and painful scenario and based upon those thoughts, I began to make a series of bad choices in regards to relationships with the opposite sex.

Since there would be no boyfriend, no husband and therefore, no children for this ugly girl, I decided that I would never allow anyone to get close enough to win my heart. I would not allow love to enter the picture because it would only mean eventual rejection. I would flirt and maybe go on a couple of dates with a guy, but never allow it to get to the point where I would have to stop hiding my prosthetic and explain what had happened to me. I wrapped my heart in Teflon and became a champion heart-breaker. I was a young lady who could flirt outrageously and there were several young men who were interested in me. I always managed to keep my body angled in such a way that my right arm remained hidden the entire time and none of my dates had a clue that I was hiding something that should have been obvious had they really been paying attention. I often wondered why they never noticed that I did everything with my left hand and never let them walk on the right side of my body so as to avoid holding my right hand.

These flirtations and short-lived relationships were, as I said previously, doomed from the beginning. I trusted no one and did whatever was humanly possible to avoid getting emotionally involved with anyone. That is, until my freshman year in college when I met a young man from Indiana who was a junior at the college I was attending. From the moment I first laid eyes on him, I somehow knew that this young man was going to change my life forever, although I didn't have a clue as to how it would happen. Initially, I couldn't wrap my head around his attraction to me and in the back of my mind questioned whether or not it was just a cruel game to him. He was gorgeous. Physically one of the best looking young men I had ever seen: tall, well-built, with beautiful blue eyes. He lived off-campus and hung out with a popular party crowd that consisted of athletes, pretty girls and rich kids. Definitely not my scene. Despite my hesitancy, in an honest conversation he admitted that his family would never accept me as his girlfriend because of the color of my skin and that he wasn't ready for anything serious. Now, I probably should have known better and walked away right then and there after that conversation. But I didn't for a couple of reasons: I still had no desire to allow myself to fall in love with anyone, so I had no problem keeping our relationship light-hearted and second, we genuinely liked each other. After knowing him for just a few months, I already valued his opinions and enjoyed his company. I was fairly certain his circle of friends had no idea that he called me every night and that we would talk for hours. Nor did they know how many times we met in hidden spots around campus, curling up together in empty class rooms, complaining about our professors, work load and general frustrations with life and laughing about our freakishly similar farm kid experiences. We became great friends, which to me, was more important than being sweethearts. I felt a level of comfort around him that I hadn't felt with anyone else on campus and in just a few months, our lives would become intertwined forever.

It was also during this time that I began to seriously question my faith and the organized religion that I had been raised to follow. During my freshman year, I went to church services each Sunday as required, but, as my social life increased in intensity, gradually started to lose interest and slowly felt the faith of my youth slipping away. My faith had already been tested with the loss of my arm and during high school; attending church became a boring obligation – despite a mission trip to the state of Washington the summer before my senior year in high school. By the time I left for college, I had little patience for God-talk. Cynicism set in for the long haul when a theology professor, whose lectures on the superiority of the Christian Reformed faith began to sound like a cult leader's ratings, continually marked all of my papers that semester with a bright red "C" and the same message written at the top of the page (also in red ink): "This is not what the Christian Reformed faith teaches. Prof. V". I had hit the brick wall of religiosity in the sense that what I was encountering at college was more about how religious a person was and less about how a person is religious (in this case, I was questioning religious doctrine). My move from a small-town to a city meant that I was meeting people from all different walks of life who practiced religions I'd only read about and lived lifestyles I never dreamed existed. I'd been taught to believe that these were the sinners who were destined for the fiery flames of hell and yet, these were some of the most spiritual people I had ever met. I was sensing that we had more in common than differences, but I couldn't reconcile the teachings of my youth with what I was hearing. This burgeoning period of questioning my faith and what I believed in opened wounds that had been festering. The protective fog that existed in my brain that had seemingly protected me from delving into the events of August 15, 1979 began to slowly dissipate. Emotions I hadn't felt in the six long years since that day began to build again and without conscious intent, my prayers became bitter lamentations: "Where were you God; so many years ago and where are you now when I am so lost?"

But the real shattering of my faith occurred on a rainy fall night in 1984 when I was date-raped by an older student on a freezing cold, hard cement bench in a dugout by the baseball field. As I lay there trying desperately to blank out the unwelcome intrusion of my body, his well-muscled arm heavy across my chest pinning me firmly into place along with the dry, painful sawing motion that felt as though my body was being torn apart, my pleas to stop ignored and my tears of pain dripping on to the collar of my pretty blouse...the last remnants of my religious faith drained out of my body along with the fluids from his. God wasn't anywhere near that dugout.

When it was over, I ran as fast as I could back to my room. I locked the door and climbed fully dressed, shoes and all into my bed. I cried until there were no tears left to cry. Not knowing what else to do, I called a girlfriend who was a sophomore living in the same dorm. She'd been a protective confidant and was much more sophisticated than I. She knew the young man, as well and knew what he was capable of. She did her best to calm me down during our brief conversation but, I was inconsolable. I left the safety of my room and sought shelter in an out of the way office on campus where I thought no one would find me. But, a couple of hours later, a young security guard, making his midnight rounds, found me curled up in a ball under a desk, shivering with cold and still very upset. He gently coaxed the story out of me and was ready to radio for campus security assistance to transport me to get medical care. I was mortified and didn't want the attention and I begged him not to tell anyone else what had happened to me. With reluctance, he finally agreed, wrapped me in a blanket and escorted me back to my room with a firm warning to go directly to the nurse's office as soon as it opened later that morning. He advised me that he would be calling me that afternoon to make sure I had seen the nurse. I was 18, alone and ashamed. I did not go to the nurse's office that day. I threw away the clothing I'd worn that night and took a long, hot shower to wash away the blood. I carried the secret of that rape for 25 years.

Obviously, the world didn't end that night and I carried on as if nothing had happened. You see, this had become the normal pattern of my life and it seemed much easier to hide than to face painful realities. So, I pushed the event as far back into the recesses of my mind as I could and slammed the door shut on the memory. Just as there was no benefit to dwelling on the loss of my limb, there was no benefit to dwelling on the brutal rape. It was over and done with and the only difference in my normal daily routine was that I now went out of my way to avoid the young man's dorm and had to find new shortcuts to use so that I could get to my classes in order to avoid running in to him. I also found that I'd gained a personal body guard in the campus security guard who had found me the night I was raped. He gave me the number to the beeper he wore at all times and for the rest of the school year, he made himself available whenever I needed an escort around campus after dark and he would leave notes of encouragement in my mailbox on a regular basis reminding me that he was just a phone call away at all times. 1984 became 1985 and before I knew it, it was May and my first year of college was over.

The summer of 1985 was spent in northern Michigan as a camp counselor at a camp supported by the Christian Reformed Church. I vaguely remembered offerings being taken at my home town church for this particular camp. It wasn't that I wanted to be a camp counselor, it was more the fact that there was no way I was going to spend my first summer of freedom in Brooten, Minnesota with my parents. I was convinced that if I did go home, I would be stuck there forever.

I completely enjoyed myself that summer and found I had very little time to feel sorry for myself in regards to my childhood when I compared it to the hardscrabble background some of the campers came from. These were kids from some of the poorest cities in Michigan, Ohio, and Indiana and they were every color of the rainbow and ranging in age 6 to 14. For most of them, this was the only opportunity they would have in their lives to attend a summer-time sleepover camp and it was my job as a camp counselor to make it a week they would never forget. It was a welcome relief to focus on the happiness of others rather than wallowing in my own pitiful problems. I found that because of my experiences as a child, it easy to relate to these children and it was a summer filled with joy and laughter. I spent my summer tromping through the woods with my groups, learned how to build a proper fire and how to cook delicious meals for 12 over a campfire. I even learned how to row a canoe and managed not to drown myself or any of my campers. I spent my weekends partying like a fool in Detroit and Chicago with fellow camp counselors and had more fun than I'd ever thought possible. But, throughout the entire summer, I hid my prosthetic arm and found creative ways to compensate if necessary. No one, with the exception of a camper or two, ever guessed and if they did, not one word was said about it to me. All too quickly, summer was over. I felt renewed and invigorated after my summer experience and I was ready to buckle down and focus on my studies during my sophomore year. I decided to major in psychology and become a social worker.

But first, there was the "End of Summer" bash that was held in late August each year for upper class students – no freshmen allowed. My girlfriends and I made our way to the party and what a party it was: literally wall to wall people. It took us a full 30 minutes to get from one side of the room to the other. As I scanned the crowd for other friends attending, my eyes met the blue eyes of my Indiana farm boy who was standing several yards away. When we finally pushed our way through the crowd to each other, he grabbed me in his arms and we hugged each other tightly, absolutely thrilled to see each other after a long summer apart. He laughingly whispered that he had been afraid I might have found someone to replace him during the summer. I happily informed him that hadn't happened and just knew that THIS was going to be a stellar year.

Lorie Tensen

PHOTOS

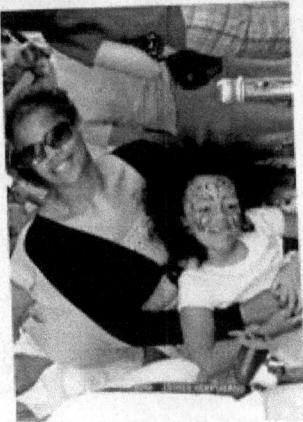

June 2014

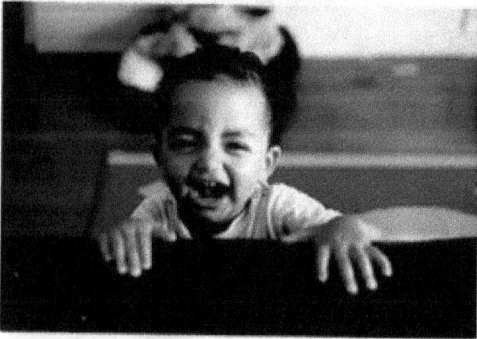

NOAH

Just a few short weeks later, after a visit to the nurse's office for a flu bug I couldn't seem to shake; I found out that I was pregnant. I was 19, hundreds of miles away from home, a sophomore at college and I had no idea what to do. Yet again: life as I knew it was over. Bad decision after bad decision. This one was a doozy.

There was no question that my religious parents would be furious and extremely disappointed with me. Aside from the high school health teacher offering up a 10-minute abbreviated version of an entire chapter explaining the differences between men and women, I had not received any sex education or information regarding my menstrual cycle for that matter as I had sporadic periods that had been affected by years of anorexia. I was self-taught and obviously, I was not a good teacher. No one could have ever accused me of being sophisticated; that is for sure. My primary fear was that mom and dad would cut off all lines of communications with me and leave me hanging in the wind all by myself. From past experience, I knew that my father could be one of the coldest, most unbending men in the world when his children disappointed him. I had seen it first hand and prayed that I wouldn't be on the receiving end of his chilly anger. My mother was definitely the more emotional parent: she yelled when she was angry. I could only imagine the scope of her anger and disappointment in me. I had also been privy to the wall of disdainful silence that she would retreat behind when she was especially angry and I knew I was in for a rough time with her, as well. I would lay in bed at night with my stomach churning just imagining the one-sided conversation that would be laced with her tears and bitter accusations that I had not only disappointed myself, but I had let down my mother, father, siblings, grandparents, cousins and worst of all, my Christian faith. I dreaded the phone call, but morning sickness very quickly became "all-day" sickness and I was forced to skip class after class because almost any type of movement brought on waves of nausea. Decisions had to be made — quickly. I called my sister-in-law and she enticed me home to Minnesota with the promise that she and my brother would help me talk to my parents and that I could live with them, if necessary. I didn't tell anyone at school that I was pregnant — not even the father of my unborn baby. My belly stayed flat until January, so, I carried on as usual, pretending nothing was amiss and that there wasn't a baby growing in my womb. In December, I sat for my exams, packed all of my belongings, wished my roommates a Merry Christmas and flew to Minnesota. Unlike my friends, however, I had no idea whether or not I would ever be returning to Michigan.

January 1986 found me safe in the bosom of my eldest brother's family. The deal I'd made with my sister-in-law was that if I agreed to return to Minnesota, she and my brother would break the news of my pregnancy to my parents and arrange a sit-down with the two of them remaining present while my mother, father and I talked. As expected, the news of my pregnancy was not received well, however, my mother and father agreed to meet with me. The evening of our sit-down, my father walked into my brother's house without a glance in my direction. He refused to participate in the conversation and sat silently in a living room chair, turning the floor over to my mother. There were harsh words, a lot of tears and no real resolution. After several hours talking in circles, we decided to call it a night. As they were leaving, my father approached me in the utility room and I braced myself for his icy words of anger but, instead, he looked me in the eye and said: "I love you and I will be there for you." I was stunned speechless. My dad always had the final say in our family and when he said that, I knew I would be welcomed home and given the support I needed. Within a week, I'd moved back home with my parents. My mother's anger and disappointment regarding my decisions were quickly forgotten and she spent the next few weeks taking care of me. Every night she would tuck me into my bed with a hug and kiss, just like she'd done when I was a small child. Despite the long road ahead of me, I was very grateful to know my parents had my back.

After much discussion, it was decided that I would move to Denver, Colorado to spend the remainder of my pregnancy with a maternal aunt and her husband who opened their home to young women who were pregnant and unwed. I fell in love with Denver. It was a beautiful city and my aunt and uncle were fantastic. He was a minister in a Christian Reformed Church and yet they were the most non-judgmental, welcoming, loving and gracious hosts. There was another young lady from Montana staying there, as well, and she was expecting her baby that March. My baby was due sometime in May and we became fast friends. These were not idyllic months: we had many fun days, but there was also an element of sadness that I carried every single day. I spent several days each week being counseled by Bethany Christian Services, an adoption agency. I had not yet decided if I would raise this baby on my own or place him for adoption. I bought a diary and every day, I tearfully wrote a love letter to my baby. I described the way I looked, my personality, my family, my favorite color, foods and animals. I tried to provide my unborn baby with every bit of information he/she might need...just in case I decided to place the baby up for adoption and he/she wanted to search for me. As my due date gets closer, I am filled with an immense and overwhelming sadness due to the decision I must make. I am torn and there is no else who can make this decision for me. Would I be able to raise a child on my own? Would it be a selfish decision to place the child for adoption and return to my studies? As an adopted child myself, how would I bear the agony of never seeing my baby again? I wrestled with these questions for months and remained unable to find the answers. My friend gave birth to a beautiful baby girl she decides to raise. On April 13, 1986 several weeks before my due date, I gave birth to a tiny 5lb 12oz baby boy. He was perfect and indescribably beautiful: with enormous brown eyes and wispy brown hair. His skin was the color of heavy cream and he was so tiny, he drowned in the newborn clothes I'd bought for him. My heart had finally been captured by a member of the male species and I fell in love for the very first time. I named my beautiful boy, Noah. He sleeps in a basket beside my bed and each night I stayed up writing in his book usually catching just an hour or two of sleep. I take pictures of him in every outfit I've bought for him. I take pictures of him sleeping and awake. I take pictures of his perfect little fingers and toes, his unblemished knees. I take pictures of him snuggled in the crook of my arm and I request doubles of each batch of film: one set for his book and one set for me. I still don't know what my decision will be, but if my choice is to allow another woman to raise my son, I will have documented every moment of our short time together.

When Noah is three days old, my mother flies to Denver to stay with me during what will be the single most agonizing 7 days of my life. I am allowed by Bethany Christian Services to keep my son with me for the first 10 days of his life and then I must release him – perhaps permanently – to the adoption agency. I will be given just 3 days after that to change my mind. I am an emotional wreck and my heart is breaking into pieces. I have never loved anyone as deeply as I already love this child and I spend every waking moment holding him in my arms: memorizing his beautiful face, his delicious baby scent and the shape of his tiny fingers and toes. He is my sweet boy. We have bonded and he snuggles against me, too young to know that these might be the last few days he and his young mother will ever snuggle again.

The awful day arrives when I must let him go. On this particular day, my heart is the body part being put through a grinder of emotions, however, this time it is ten times worse. I pack his tiny clothes, numerous baby blue blankets and the diary in a box. I fill one more camera with pictures and then I curl up in my bed, with my body wrapped around his tiny one, staring into his big brown eyes. Upstairs, I hear the doorbell ring and I know its Ann from Bethany. She's here to take my Noah. Seconds later, the doorbell rings again. This time, it's a floral delivery. My sister, Jody knowing what a crushing day this will be for me, has sent flowers along with a message of support and love. I kiss my Noah once more – possibly for the last time ever – and gently place him into Ann's arms and then I run to my own mother's waiting arms and sob until long after Ann's car pulls away. It is over. Now, I have just three short days to make a decision about whether or not this will be a permanent placement. I am determined to make a mature and well informed decision. So I spend the next few days going over every option available. I read countless profiles of couples who wish to adopt my tiny boy. I cry an ocean of tears and get very little sleep. The day before my flight home to Minnesota, I am finally able to make a decision that I know in my heart is best for Noah and me.

MOTHERHOOD AND MARRIAGE

On May 10, my mother, Noah and I, board a plane to Minnesota. I have been 20 for three days and am now a single parent. Noah and I spend the next couple of months living with my parents. Even though I knew the road ahead would be a difficult one, I was happier than I'd been in years. I made a conscious decision to raise this child and I had to focus all my energy on being the best parent I could be. There was now a tiny boy depending on me for everything and I couldn't allow having a prosthetic limb to slow me down. I had to think about our future and how I would provide for us, so, I made the decision to return to Grand Rapids so that I could finish my degree. I still had a decent amount of money in my bank account from my insurance settlement and I hoped that this money would last until I graduated from college and found a job. I was so naive: determined to raise my son on my own without the help of my parents who had generously offered to let us live with them. My mother offered to babysit for me while I worked towards an Associate's degree at a community college located in Willmar, Minnesota. My concern was that I would not be able to find a job if I stayed in the area. I didn't feel I could physically handle a job as in the fields of study available the community college: it would be a bit awkward to work as a one-handed dental assistant or nurse! I believed that the best option for me was to finish my BSW in Michigan and so, at the end of May, Noah and I moved back to Grand Rapids.

I found an apartment about a half mile from the school and registered for full-time first semester classes and had made it back to Grand Rapids just in time to sneak into a last minute opening in an 8-week accelerated summer session that began towards the end of June. I hired an energetic high school baby sitter who babysat for a young couple who lived and worked on-campus. I'd met them during my freshman year and babysat for their children on occasion and they had become good friends of mine. They numbered among a very select few who were privy to the fact that I had returned to school as a single parent. They also helped me arrange for another sitter who lived just across the street from the college and whose husband was attending Seminary School at the same college. This second sitter would take over when the high school student went back to school in the fall. I was all set to go. Noah was now a couple of months old and I felt completely at ease going to class every day because I knew his sitter (with occasional help from her mom) was taking good care of him. Back on campus grounds once again, I found myself running into old friends who were naturally curious as to why I'd disappeared for 9 months and then just as suddenly, reappeared. I had no desire to let people into my business and always managed to change the subject. My focus had indeed changed: all I wanted to do now was go to class and then hurry home to my baby at the end of the day. We lived in a cozy apartment and there was nothing I enjoyed more than spending time with my baby boy. Socializing was the last thing on my mind. By the time first semester started, however, my secret was out. One afternoon, as I was heading out of the library, a young man and woman who were casual acquaintances I'd met through my son's father, cornered me and advised me that knew exactly why I had disappeared. They informed me that someone had seen me with a baby and that somehow; pictures had been taken of my son and passed along to his father. Indiana Farm Boy was looking for me. On a crisp fall afternoon, he found me. I hear my name being called from across the campus square and there he is. He pulls me into his arms and swings me around in circles. He finally sets me down and without releasing me, asks me why I had disappeared so many months before. I start to lie and he shakes his head at me. "Be honest," he says "because I know the truth. Tell me what my son's name is." He is surprisingly not angry with me. He allows me to explain in detail what I have been through since the previous August and he tells me, rightly so, that I have been selfish by not including him in this monumental decision. I agree, of course, and assure him that I have no intentions of forcing him to be a father. He is a senior with big plans and because I excluded him from all decision making, he should not feel obligated towards me. I beg him not to begin a relationship with our tiny son. After all, he will be leaving the state in May and how would we manage visits with a small child when dad is hundreds of miles away? He agrees, with the understanding that I will give him weekly updates and provide him with pictures of Noah on a regular basis. He feels no real connection to his child and as he is only 22 years old himself, admits that he is somewhat relieved that I am not pressuring him. We are both happy with this decision and continue this arrangement until he graduates from college and moves to the East Coast.

When I think back on that time, I realize how selfish I was and how immature we both were. The decisions we made were thought up by two college kids who felt they were acting in the best interest of the child they had created and for themselves. We still cared very deeply for one another and considered ourselves friends, but we knew we were headed in different directions. We continued to exchange letters and pictures several times a year. There was no anger, no animosity and no regrets between the two of us because what we did worked for us: I was still a college student and he was on the cusp of what would eventually turn into an amazing career. Our plan was to continue along in this manner and gradually open the lines of communication as Noah got older. When Noah was old enough, we would figure out a way for him to spend time on the East Coast with his father. But time and distance can ruin even the best intentions. We were still young and still selfish. Both of us were in serious relationships with the people we would eventually marry. So, we met one last time in the city where he was living and after a heartbreaking weekend trying to figure out what was best for our child, decided the right thing to do was to leave well enough alone until Noah turned 18. Noah was already attached to the man I was dating and adding another person into the mix at his young age would have just been confused him. Gradually, all communication ceased. Sadly, he passed away when our son was a teenager and they were never able to meet in person and build a relationship.

My life as a young single parent was difficult and exhausting. I made a valiant attempt to go back to college full time to finish my degree. I paid the bills and tuition with money left over from the insurance settlement. My parents, being of the school of thought that one should work for a living, had accepted the first offer given by their insurance company for my accident. This money was originally intended to cover the cost of my prosthetic repairs until I reached the age of 21. When I was 16, I was taken to the local bank, given a bank book which contained what looked like a small fortune to a teenager and told that I was now in charge of my living expenses. I received no financial tutoring on how to manage this rather large sum and spent quite a bit of the money frivolously for the next three years. Aside from a small student loan, I also used the money to pay for my college tuition, books and living expenses. By the time I became a mother, there was very little left. I quickly learned that the cost of raising a child was quite considerable and spent the first year eating crackers and peanut butter in order to afford baby formula and diapers. In addition to going to school full time, I worked a 3rd shift job stuffing ads in newspapers just to make ends meet. Finally, my schedule and lack of sleep became too much for me I was forced to drop out of college and decided to work full-time. When my son was three years old, I suffered my first bout of serious depression and something in the tone of my voice during a phone call to my parents had my mother packing her bags and on her way to Grand Rapids within hours to take care of Noah and myself as I was too physically and mentally exhausted to properly care for either of us. It was one of the few times I had asked my parents for help and I was very grateful that she made the trip without hesitation. Despite the difficult first few years together, there were never any regrets about the decision to become a single parent at such a young age. My little boy had stolen my heart the moment he was born and I was ready to give up my life for him and quite determined to be the best parent I could be. Today, even though he is a handsome, strong young man in his late 20s, making his own way in life, my mother's eyes see a skinny little boy with big brown eyes and freckles who continues to melt my heart.

During this hectic period of my life, I met the man I would eventually marry. Despite having had boyfriends and giving birth, I still felt I would never find true love with anyone who would accept me completely, and experience a grand romance that would lead to marriage. I believed that I would never be able to provide my son with a happy family life and possibly, siblings. I had insulated myself so completely from loving anyone with the exception of my son Noah and I was well aware that no one stood a chance of ever winning a piece of my heart. We met through a mutual friend when I was 21 and he was just 8-months older. I thought he was annoying and it got on my nerves that he stared at me the entire night. He was persistent and I agreed to go out with him. On our first date, I took my son along in his stroller because I figured we were a package deal. He accepted the challenge and we spent the next six tempestuous years in an on-and-off again relationship. When he proposed, it was in the midst of a period when we had broken up with each other. I had made up my mind that this time, our break up was for good, but he was convinced that if I just gave him one more chance, he would be the best boyfriend I could ever have; in fact, he would show his commitment by marrying me. I was mentally exhausted after years of on-and-off drama and felt that I was not being a good parent by allowing this man to continue to come in and out of my life. My son adored him and he, despite his immaturity, adored my son. So, while it pains me to admit, I decided to marry him not because I loved him and we were ready for marriage, but because I felt that this time he was going to make a serious effort to make our relationship work, after all – he had never been willing to make a total commitment in the 6 years we had dated – even when we had lived together. This time, he said, he would put our life together before fun times with his friends and he would treat me with the respect I deserved. I convinced myself that once we had made that ultimate commitment, I would feel secure enough to let down my guard and trust him to treasure my wounded soul. He was the first man who had ever proposed to me and despite our many issues; he hadn't run away when he heard my story. I would learn to love him over time. I would finally be able to build a family with someone! So we called our respective families and married in front of a judge the summer of 1992. It was not the best day I'd ever had. I'm quite sure he'd agree. My parents got lost and were upset with me, we were broke because we had spent money we didn't have and I couldn't shake the feeling that I had just made a terrible mistake.

Our marriage limped along for 18 years. The first year was the best: I ignored the stress that was building inside of me. I knew I was depressed, but I thought if I just made more of an effort, I would eventually snap out of it. So, we set up house in a historical neighborhood, in a large apartment that took up half of a beautiful old house. We added a whippet puppy, named Elvis, to our family and then a cat that we named Pudding and considered our second – and very spoiled - child. Noah was thrilled to officially have a dad and my husband seemed happy, as well. But, I was at the beginning of a downward spiral into chronic depression and as the years passed, I continued to feel as though I was carrying the weight of the world sitting on my shoulders. I didn't know anything about depression and castigated myself repeatedly for not being a better wife. I could not figure out why my heart felt completely void of any feelings for this man and felt terrible knowing that because I'd become such an expert at hiding my emotions, he happily went to sleep by my side each night thinking all was well. So, I have to give credit where credit is due: he was a willing father to my son and loved him nearly as much as I did. He is the father of my beautiful daughter and it is because of our children that when I discuss the failure of my marriage, I do so in the context of how my accident affected every decision I made in my life and nothing else.

Marriage, as I knew very well, should not be entered into lightly. I did not take my vows lightly, but I entered into it knowing that I could not love this man the way a spouse deserved to be loved. It was my reticence at the time, not his, because I knew he loved me very much. I did feel that he was my best friend and he was the first man that I felt comfortable sharing my deep-ceded feelings of low self-esteem, ugliness, anger, bitterness and sadness. Despite my insecurities and depression and his frustrating immaturity at times, we managed to stay together until Noah was approximately 10 years old. After 9 years of living together, I knew myself well enough to know that I was never going to be happy as his wife. I felt emotionally unavailable when it came to anyone other than my son and knew I simply had nothing left for my husband, So, we separated and he moved to an apartment with the intention (on my part) of getting a divorce. After nearly three years of living apart, while both of us had moved on as far as dating others, neither of us had found the energy to file for divorce. I was happier on my own, but I was scared. My old fears reared their ugly head and I allowed myself to be convinced that no one would ever love me the way this man did. Despite my trepidation, I agreed to give the marriage another try and we reconciled in 1996. Once again, immediately after he moved back into our home, I knew I had made another big mistake. I could not bear to have him touch me and the little things became big things that tore apart our marriage. We began to bicker and there was a new snarkiness in the tones we used when arguing and the words we used became sharper. Old wounds were reopened and blame became the name of the game. We hid our discontent from everyone and our families, who were delighted that we had decided not to throw away years of a relationship, began to pressure us to have another child. My husband and I finally sat down and discussed the state of our marriage. We had made the decision to make our marriage work and neither of us was making a good effort. Perhaps a child would unite us. One night, I had a vivid dream that rocked me to my core: in my dream, a little girl wearing a school type uniform, with long chocolatey auburn hair that was naturally curly, a cleft chin and skin that was creamy and fair. She appeared to be around the age of 4. She looked me straight in the eye and said: "I'm not ready to come just yet, but I'm on my way and I'll be there soon." The dream was so real, I shook my husband awake and told him about the dream I had just had. Still shaken later that morning, I called my mother and told her about the dream. It was so real, it didn't feel like a dream as much as it did a vision. I was convinced that someday, I would give birth to a daughter.

We tried for a full year before my doctor advised me that he had put the name of a fertility doctor in my file and when we were ready, he would talk about the possibility of in vitro fertilization. Part of me felt it was a sign from the gods that we were not meant to be together after all. But, an even bigger part of me longed for a second child even though I knew it was wrong to try to "fix" an unhappy marriage by adding a new baby to the mix. But, then there was my dream...we convinced ourselves that having a baby was the right thing to do. We agreed to stop trying and to start focusing on repairing our still-broken marriage. If a pregnancy was meant to be, it would happen without the help of science. Within a month, I was pregnant.

REMINGTON

At the first ultrasound, the technician asked if we wanted to know the sex of our baby. I told her I already knew I was going to have a girl. We hadn't even discussed any boy names because I was convinced I had already met my daughter. However, I told the technician to go ahead check for herself. Sure enough, there was a little girl in my womb. I was right. We were going to have a daughter and she was due on Christmas Day.

It was a rough pregnancy. My doctor told me he had never seen such an active in utero fetus and I would often entertain my co-workers by letting them watch my burgeoning tummy wiggle and jump as she twisted and turned. My marriage was still on the rocks: during my first trimester, things were so bad, I begged my husband to agree to a divorce before she was born. He convinced me that he would make an effort to be a more supportive husband if I just hung in there. He did and I did, as well. By my 28th week, I was put on partial bed-rest due to early contractions. By my 31st week of pregnancy, I was confined to full bed rest. The weekend after Thanksgiving, I was given the all clear that that fetus was viable and if I went into labor, nothing would be done to stop it. On November 29, I went into full nesting mode and decided to rake the leaves in the front yard. At 2 am, November 30, I was in labor and headed to the hospital. Noah was 13 and old enough to make the decision about whether or not he would watch his sister come into the world. He was still undecided at that very early hour and would meet us at the hospital with his own personal labor coach. As usual, my daughter proved she already had a strong will. All labor activity stopped as our girl seemingly decided she was no longer in a hurry joins us. Finally, nearly 13 hours later, our daughter was born, with her brother happily snapping pictures of her birth.

She took my breath away. She had thick, dark chocolate brown-auburn hair, very pale skin and a cleft chin just like her dad's. I took one look at her and knew exactly what she would look like when she turned 4. I recognized this child from my dream and knew she was a gift from God. I also almost immediately had the strange thought flash through my mind that she was here in my arms on loan and that I was just her caretaker – she was a child who would belong to many. It was an uncomfortable thought to have just moments after she had entered our lives.

Just as my son had captured my heart at his birth, this newest child of mine stole my very soul. I had been given a second opportunity to experience a love unlike any other. To this day, my daughter and I are blessed to have a connection that runs deeper than most mother/daughter relationships and this has allowed us to blessedly bypass the angst-filled teenage years. Our relationship almost seems too easy at times, especially when I hear stories of the screaming and yelling that occurs in the households of friends who also have daughters her age. Oh and just a little note that relates back to my dream: she wears a uniform for school every day.

What made me especially sensitive about my relationship with my daughter from day one was the fact that I began to watch for parallels to my own childhood. I had flashbacks of my life as a young girl and knew I had to be strong enough not to transfer the weight of my past on her shoulders. I knew the chances of her losing a limb were slim to none, but feelings of loneliness, low self-esteem and the fear that no one will understand what you are going through, are traps anyone can fall in to and once you are caught up in those feeling, it's a struggle to escape. I really thought about the type of parent I wanted to be as the mother of a daughter. My son had a laid back personality and he and I developed our own distinct relationship. I could mother him, lavish him with love and affection, provide structure and discipline, but as a woman, I couldn't relate to the childhood and teenage angst that he went through as a male. He and I had an easy, open relationship and he knew he could talk to me about anything. Having a daughter of my own really brought my relationship with my own mother to the forefront. I began to examine my feelings for my own parents – especially my mother – and realized that while I loved them because I was supposed to love them, I had felt no real connection with them from the age of 13 until I was in my 30s. I rarely spoke with them and when I did, it was generally on a major holiday or birthday. My accident had created a gulf between us that I still didn't understand and did not know how to bridge and I promised myself that this would never occur between me and my children.

Unfortunately, the birth of my daughter did nothing to repair the rift between my husband and myself. We grew further apart as the years went by and I continued to suffer from chronic depression (especially after my father died in 2005) even while I pasted on a mask of perfect wife, mother and hostess for friends, family and the rest of the world. No one would have guessed just how unhappy we really were.

Because my husband was able to support us comfortably with his salary, I was fortunate to be a stay-at-home mom. I am eternally grateful for this opportunity because it allowed my relationship with my children to flourish. I was available to them every day, all day, and I happily prepared home-made meals and nutritious snacks every day. Mothering was the only area I felt I excelled at and I worked hard at it. Meanwhile, my OCD tendencies and depression had become so bad: each morning, after my children left for school, I would spend four hours cleaning our home located in a historical neighborhood of Grand Rapids. The house had hardwood floors on both floors and I would sweep, vacuum, mop (on my hands and knees) and vacuum a second time before I was satisfied no one's socks would walk across my floors and get dirty. I would spend an hour polishing the vast amount of stainless steel in my kitchen – bending so that I was eye-level with my counter tops to see if I had left and smears. Bathrooms would be disinfected from top to bottom and even the grocery items in the pantry organized with labels turned to the front. After another hour spent doing laundry and making sure all the clothes in my closet were arranged by color, sleeve and pant leg length, I would climb back into bed absolutely exhausted until five minutes before I had to do the afternoon school run. It was a vicious cycle that occurred every single day. I was mentally drained and physically worn out. My husband was worried for my emotional state because in the privacy of our home, it became very clear that I could no longer keep up the dual roles I was playing. Physically, I was slim to the point of anorexia again and the bones of my hips and clavicles were as sharp as knives. My skin was pale and drawn and I began to experience significant medical issues. My closet started to consist of items that were the same color: black, which made me look even skinnier and sicklier. I had also really begun to dread interacting with folks outside of my inner circle and felt the stirrings of agoraphobia. It took a pep talk to force myself out of my home each day beyond the drop-off and pick-up of my children. After years of barely living, I realized I could no longer continue to live my life in such a state. My husband was worried, my children were worried and friends and family were beginning to express concern, as well.

I knew that it was time to face the demons I had been living with for the past 30 years of my life. I was afraid of what I knew would be a long, difficult and very painful process but, my depression had advanced to weekly thoughts of suicide and I realized it was now or never. I was very scared of what I might discover about myself...perhaps I would discover that I truly was a difficult, unlovable person. Perhaps I simply did not have the capacity to love anyone besides my children. I made up a list of questions that I might possibly be forced to answer: What if I really did blame my parents for the accident that caused the loss of my right arm and if I did, what if the therapist told me I had to confront my parents as part of my healing process. My parents were in their 70s. Could I live with myself if it damaged our relationship irreparably? If I did have to speak with my parents, would they tell my siblings and would I lose them, as well?

Would I be told that I was simply a weak person who had allowed herself to become mired in the quicksand of self-pity? The answers I came up with were not pretty.

THE FLOODGATES OPEN

In late 2004, I began therapy. Jean, my therapist, initially listened quietly as I bemoaned the state of my marriage (I used my marriage as the basis of my unhappiness). She was the perfect professional over the course of several sessions: asking obvious questions and sending me out the door at the end of my 55 minutes with a word or two of advice. Until one day, about a month into our weekly sessions, she interrupted me mid-sentence and asked in a very matter of fact manner: "So, we've talked a lot about everything but the elephant in the room. When are we going to talk about your right arm?" My skin prickled with hot embarrassment that she had so rudely brought up a topic that as a therapist, she should KNOW was sensitive, right? Wasn't it rude of her? But, then that hot embarrassment turned into the icy sweat of someone who's been caught in big lie. The people in my life had become accustomed to ignoring the obvious. Perhaps they might make an initial inquiry, but my obvious reluctance to share the gruesome details was a broad enough hint to drop the subject. Jean was a savvy therapist and had my number from the very beginning. She bluntly told me that it was very obvious to her that every decision I had made since August 1979 had been predicated on the fact that I had never properly addressed the traumatic accident that had changed my life forever so many years ago. My ability to deftly maneuver my body in a way that shielded my right arm from public view did not go unnoticed by Jean. She gave me a verbal list of the many ways I physically found a way to hide my prosthetic and accurately described the mental fencing I did when confronted with the topic. She pointed out that when I had given her an abbreviated version of my story, it was as if I was narrating a story that had happened to someone else. There was very little emotion or inflection in my tone during the narrative and she could tell it made me physically uncomfortable dwelling on the topic once I'd finished. Any words and expressions of horror and sympathy were very quickly brushed off with a joke or I would state that it "wasn't a big deal anymore". As an experienced professional, she was the first person who was able to catch that brief moment before I started my accident-spiel, when I briefly closed my eyes, drew a breath and in that very brief moment, mentally removed myself from the story. Oh, she was very good indeed. Over the years, I had become a quick-change artist with no one else discovering the secret. I had become so adept that several of my friends admitted that it had taken those months before they learned I had a prosthetic right arm. Nearly 100% of the people who did know would share with me that they treated me the way I had taught them to treat me: like it was no big deal. Few people knew the very real and devastating lasting impact the experience had on my life.

Jean was the first person who didn't hesitate to push me to my limits when it came to confronting my feelings about what had happened to me at the tender age of 13 and just like a child confronted with a task they don't want to complete, I balked and stubbornly dug in my heels. I spent several more sessions discussing everything but the elephant in the room. Every day she patiently listened and quietly waited for my walls to crumble. Finally, one afternoon, in the midst of a diatribe about the many ways my husband had frustrated me the previous evening, I interrupted myself and angrily bit out: "I have never cried about my accident since the moment my arm went through that damned grinder. I have not allowed myself to feel genuine emotions for years because it's long over and there is nothing I can do about it. I certainly will not give myself permission to cry now, 25 years later!"

Jean looked me in the eye and very gently unlatched the gate of 25 years of bottled up pain and emotion. She simply said: "Lorie, I'm giving you permission to cry."

The floodgates were open: I cried hours for that 13 year old child who had had her arm ground to a pulp in the auger of a meat grinder. I cried for the little girl who was told over and over again to be strong and silent. Who had continually been told to hold her tears and fearfulness inside because others were hurting more than she and if she crumbled, so would they. I cried for the adolescent who was just beginning to blossom into a teenager, the girl who was embarrassed to tears because her top was being cut off by a man and her nakedness would then be exposed. I cried for the girl who was bewildered by all of the attention shown to her just because she had experienced hell on earth. I cried for the girl who missed her first day as a 7th grader in the high school building. I cried for the girl who had walked through a strange town with a metal hook hanging from her sleeve. I cried for the teenager who believed that she was a monster who needed to become a clown in order to distract attention from her fake plastic arm. I cried for the teenager who felt she had to starve herself hoping she would eventually disappear altogether. I cried for the college student who sought the wrong attention - any attention - from men because she felt she was too ugly inside and out to be loved enough by someone who would want to marry her. I cried for the young woman who agonized over whether or not she would be the best choice of parent for the child she had just given birth to. I cried for the young single mother who stubbornly refused to ask for assistance from anyone as she struggled to make ends meet and provide for her child. I cried for the woman who married a man she could never love because she still didn't have the courage to love herself. I cried for the mother who poured herself into making sure her children received all the love, affection and attention she was able to give while at the same time, she ignored her health and the world that was crumbling down around her. I cried for the grown woman who had no idea how to dream. I cried for the real Lorie Tensen who had missed out on years of closeness with the parents who had chosen her to be their Black-eyed Susabelle.

I cried a lifetime of tears in front of Jean and she never passed judgment. She had provided the opening I needed to confront my past and in doing so, empowered me. I found the strength I needed to rebuild my life. And by the time our sessions together had ended, I caught a glimpse of the little-girl lost. She was finally ready to reappear. I knew I had a lot of work to do and years of therapy ahead of me before I was ready to go it alone. Jean referred me to a psychiatrist named David, who walked with me on the next part of my journey. David was just as blunt as Jean. He not only provided me with much needed antidepressants and prescription sleep-aids so that I could finally get more than two hours of sleep each night, he also lent a sympathetic ear and a no-holds barred opinion of my life. It was time to rebuild my life, he told me. Time to invite the little-girl lost in 1979 to come back home and to finish the healing process.

David was not the type of psychiatrist who nodded his head like a bobble-headed dog while scribbling notes on a pad of paper, and sending me on my way with a prescription. After several sessions spent dissecting my life, he bluntly informed me that staying in my unhappy marriage was slowly killing me and that it was time for me to file for divorce. He stated me that it was time to reassess the direction my life was headed and figure out what I wanted to do. My children were growing up and would soon be leaving my nest. I had no plan, no direction. No idea of what I wanted to do with my time once they were on their own. He helped me to understand what had taken place in my mind in the moments that immediately followed the accident. The physical pain had been so intense the only way my mind was able to shut it out was to create a mental state that became long-term in which I was able to disassociate from the pain of the trauma. The girl who existed in this mental state was able to mentally rise above the intense pain and view the scene as though she were watching it happen to someone else. Disassociating myself, created a memory block, oh – I remembered the pain, of course, but for decades, I blocked out the memories of the little girl who had existed before August 15, 1979. My physical self-remained, but the innocence was gone and my mind protected myself from further pain, by inserting a non-penetrable wall armor around both my emotional being. Being continually told not to cry and to keep my emotions to myself also added a psychological barrier forced on to my person by outsiders. Without proper counseling that should have occurred immediately, I was not only physically scarred by my accident, but mentally and emotionally damaged, as well. My ability to make appropriate emotional decisions was stunted. I turned off those feelings. I added to that by pummeling my self-esteem mercilessly. I wasn't emotionally capable of wading through the muck to see the reality of who I was: I was still me. Still a beautiful girl. Somewhat battered and bruised, but alive. Instead, I didn't receive counseling and was left to navigate on my own from the age of 13 until I imploded in my 30s.

These sessions were grueling and very painful times. I met with David for weekly sessions that lasted over five long years. There were several layers of protection that had been built over time which needed to be peeled off and exposed one layer at a time. I learned quite a bit about post-traumatic stress disorder that occurs after a traumatic event and how it manifests itself in children and teenagers. Three of the most interesting facts I learned, were that: 1) girls are more likely than boys to get PTSD, 2) teens are more likely than younger children or adults to show impulsive and aggressive behaviors and 3) children and teens that have gone through trauma often have other types of problems. I had spent years beating myself up for some of the decisions I had made along the way. I struggled on a daily basis with my inability to be emotionally available my entire teenage and adult life. I knew the love I had for my children was real and pure, but when it came to feeling anything real, emotionally, for everyone else, there was nothing left to give. I certainly went through the motions, said the words, and felt affection towards many people in my life, but in reality, there was no substance behind any of the affectionate words that came out of my mouth. I wanted to feel emotion. I wanted to love and believe in the love that other offered me. But, I couldn't.

By the summer of 2008, I knew what the two most important steps were that I needed to take in order to start the rebuilding phase of my healing process.

The first major decision I made was to file for divorce. I was 42 when I filed and 44 when it was finalized. My divorce was ugly, messy and extremely contentious. But, it was the only choice I felt I could make that would give both of us another chance to find happiness. There are many who disagreed with my decision to end our marriage, because to those on the outside our relationship, while distant, seemed fine. But, there were only two opinions that mattered, that of my children. They were sad, of course, initially. But they had both spent years watching me suffer from deep depression and were both mature enough to sense that my survival meant letting go of my past in order to find my future and that meant divorcing their dad. There was a sense of polite coldness that existed in our house. My husband and I did not scream at each other or call each another awful names what we did was much worse: nothing. We lived on separate floors in our home. I had to walk away. I was still making mistakes, however, and didn't go about it the right way. He had his own issues, but I take full responsibility for my part in the messy break-up of our life together.

What I have come to realize through both therapy and self-discovery is that in addition to my emotional issues, we were simply two very different people. We probably could have sputtered along for a few more years, but eventually, the marriage would have ended in divorce no matter what. Our dreams and goals in life were completely at odds with one another and we had nothing more to talk about. He very quickly moved on and has remarried a woman who shares his ideas about what is important in life and whose values match his. This actually allowed me to release any remaining feelings of guilt I had retained regarding the ending of my marriage. Hindsight has given me clarity and in the aftermath, I am finally able to remember the good times: the many moments of laughter, passion and friendship. Although I know that we will never be friends again (for reasons that are between the two of us), we do our best to co-parent the two wonderful children we share.

The second decision I made was to finally obtain my college degree. I registered for full-time classes in the spring of 2008 and entered college for the second time in my life in August 2008. I studied diligently, wrote papers that seemed to flow from somewhere deep within and aced nearly every final exam. On December 15, 2010, I graduated from college with a Bachelor of Science degree in psychology and a GPA I was very proud of. That same afternoon, I received a large envelope in the mail that contained my divorce decree: signed and finalized on December 15, 2010. It was a day that was both the happiest and one of the saddest days of my life - a beginning and an end.

DISCOVERING LORIE

There are lessons in life that are more difficult and painful than others. My life has been a non-stop learning experience and I continue to learn more about myself each day. During the years of self-discovery, I was also able to reconnect with my faith. It was no longer the faith of my younger self; it was more - much more. I studied Buddhism and spirituality searching for an unknown *something* until discovering at last that my faith in life and humanity, my spirituality, begins within me. It is not a deity, a specific religion or church, rather, it is the knowledge that light, love, and truth begins within my heart. The key to this epiphany was forgiveness - not the forgiveness of those around me - but the forgiveness of myself. I could spend the rest of my life searching for some*thing* or some*one* I could dump my blame and anger on. I did spend way too many years on that particular path to no avail....when really what I needed to do was to search within my own heart and soul. Of course it was unfair for me to have gone through such a traumatic accident. Yes, there were instances that could and should have been handled in a different manner. But my accident was a shock for all the members of my family and it affected each and every one of us in many different ways.

So, in order to begin the process of healing, I forgave myself first. I had come very close to eliminating the little girl who had her arm amputated in 1979. I had forced myself to be strong and resilient and tried hard not to allow any cracks in my facade. I mentally kicked myself on a regular basis when weakness reared its wobbly head. Eventually, I became a much hardened version of that mentally disassociated child. I was finally able to forgive myself for the punishment I had put myself through for more than 30 years and when I did, I felt true joy and the warmth of the love I knew I was capable of giving and receiving. Forgiving my self-opened my eyes and softened my heart. It allowed me to reflect upon my past experiences with not only forgiveness, but real empathy, compassion and understanding towards any and all whom I had sub-consciously held accountable for the trauma I had endured so many years ago. Forgiving myself gave permission for that little-girl lost to finally come home.

As a parent, I cannot begin to fathom the agony that my parents experienced that awful day in 1979. I was their Black-eyed Susabelle, their much-loved little brown doll and I know now they felt helpless in the face of their daughter's unimaginable pain. Their love for me never diminished, never faltered, never wavered. They continually offered their support in the only ways they knew how. My accident did not stop the world from turning on its axis: there were bills to pay, a store to run, new daughters-and-sons-in-law, grandchildren to celebrate, welcome and love. I am blessed to be a member of this strong family. During the last 10 years of his life, my father became nearly unrecognizable...in a wonderful way. He was warm, emotional and physically demonstrative in a way he had never been before. I looked forward to my calls home because he usually answered the telephone and would spend the first five minutes giving me the low-down on the current Minnesota weather forecast. Every conversation ended with words of love and when he died in 2005, he died knowing I loved him with every fiber of my being.

Then there is my mother. Writing this book would not have been possible without the love and support of my mom. For over 30 years we had tiptoed around each other. Never daring to discuss the past, not wanting to reopen old wounds. Our awkwardness around each other was obvious to me and I grew up thinking she didn't know how to love me anymore. I felt abandoned by her and I resented her. When I started writing this book, it occurred to me that she and I were the only ones who truly knew what had happened at 6:18 pm, August 15, 1979. I needed to hear her side of the story. I told myself that I wanted the story to be accurate. What I heard changed my relationship with my mother forever. My mother spent 30 years in her own personal hell. During our many discussions, I found out that she blamed herself for the loss of my right arm and that every time she saw me, she could only see the damage she thought she had caused and she could not face me. She interpreted my rebellion and distance as a sign that I blamed her, as well, and she was so wracked with guilt that she did not feel she had the right to mother me the way I deserved.

I was stunned. Yes, I had felt emotionally abandoned and longed for the security of my mother's arms, but not once did I blame her. I had always known that it was a terrible accident: a mother heard her wounded child screaming hysterically, she came running to my rescue and flipped the switch to turn off the machine that was causing her child so much pain. It was an accident. Blinded by my own emotional struggles, I could not see that she was suffering, too. We spent many months having intense discussions via the telephone. She insisted that she did not know how I could ever forgive her and how I could love her. To this I replied then and I will proclaim for the rest of our lives: there is nothing to forgive. As for loving this woman: in 1966, I was brought into this world by another woman so that I could become Doris Tensen's daughter. I am her Black-eyed Susabelle and she is my mom, who I love with all of my heart.

I also feel blessed to have had the experience of growing up as a member of a small Midwestern farming community - a community that provided unconditional support to my family and especially to me during that extremely difficult summer so many years ago. I witnessed this outpouring of love and support again when my father died in July 2005. He was a much loved and well-known figure in my home town and the lines of visitors at the viewing and packed church at his funeral was heart-warming to witness. My mother, siblings and I will never forget that.

So my 30-year journey has taken me full circle and I finally feel I have matured into the woman I was meant to be. The little-girl lost has finally been found and while it has been a long and arduous journey I have survived with a renewed sense of hope for the future.

It is now June 2014 and I am 48 years old. Every morning, rain or shine, winter or summer, I start my day with a smile and give thanks for a new day. The clothes in my closet are as bright as a box of crayons. The body that wears this clothing is healthy and strong. The wrinkles that developed around my eyes and mouth caused by years of negativity and stress have virtually disappeared and my skin has become unblemished and smooth for the first time in many years. Although, I admit that I happily look forward to the creases and wrinkles caused by laughter and old age that will someday be carved all over my face. My heart bursts with gratitude that there are so many wonderful people in my life. But, I am especially grateful for my children.

Twice, through the dark clouds of my existence, I was presented with a light to find my way and those lights are named Noah and Remington. I have never loved the way I am able to love my children. So many parents say this about their children but, for me especially, they have been remarkable gifts of unconditional love. Despite my own many issues, when it came to being a good parent, I was somehow able to shove the darkness aside with a strength and confidence I could muster for nothing else. Turns out being an amputee has nothing to do with ones ability to parent and while I'm definitely not in line to win the Parent of the Year award, I know I'm the type of parent I set out to be. We laugh, we cry, we hug and we kiss. We talk about everything and my kids are well aware that mom is their strongest champion. My children know the details of my life story and they were first-hand witnesses of my struggle to cope during the dark years of my depression. They were also first-hand witnesses the brightest days: when I no longer took anti-depressants and persevered through the break-up of my marriage and when I walked across the stage to receive my college diploma. In the eyes of my children, I am the Bionic Woman: I am not broken, I am not disabled and I am not weak. Noah and Remy continue to be my strongest sources of support and the sunshine that carries me through any periods of darkness and self-doubt that reappear.

LOVE, LOVE, LOVE

Oh, the joys of dating after a failed marriage and as a woman-of-a-certain age! What I know for sure is that I have made a conscious choice not to remarry until I am truly ready and yes, some day I would like to be a wife again. I still suffer from low self-esteem and have always felt less-than. Not by society's standards of beauty, but my own. From the age of 13, after my accident, I had believed my prosthetic arm made me unattractive and that no man would ever look at me and see *me* and not the plastic right arm that hung by my side. I was unable to give credit to myself for being an interesting person and quite honestly, never gave my poor suitors enough credit that was capable of deciding whether or not they wanted to build a relationship with me. I actually had physical reactions whenever I imagined having to wear short sleeves around a partner or heaven forbid – be naked with a lover. My stomach would cramp and I would nearly hyperventilate at the thought. It was years before I walked around in sleeveless shirts around my former husband and in fact, during the 23 years I was with my husband, the only time he saw me without my prosthetic was by accident!

There is always that moment in the relationship, usually 2-3 months in, when I have no choice but to tell a potential partner that I am missing a limb. Unless you've lived through that moment, you cannot imagine the awkwardness of that moment. One gentleman told me he felt deeply offended and somewhat betrayed that I had kept it a secret for so long. I tried to explain the reasons why from my point of view, but it was not enough. So, after the first serious relationship that made it past the 3-month story-telling ended, I took a long hiatus to re-evaluate the type of partner I required and deserved in my life and the list of must-have's was long. My friends insisted that any man who rejected me based upon the fact that I wore a prosthetic wasn't worth my time.

But it wasn't just about my potential partner: it was more about me and the importance of discovering the type of person I had become. I no longer wanted to constantly be on guard. My newly discovered true-self wasn't the woman my former husband had lived with: she had been a hard woman. Always on the defensive, always tired, always in physical pain, always busy. The woman I had become was much softer. I laughed with ease, grew my hair out, had surgery to rid myself of physical pain that had plagued me for decades and discovered a new-found energy and zest for life. I also discovered humility. I realized that in order to move forward, I had to study the mistakes I had made in my failed marriage and not only acknowledge those mistakes, but figure how to learn from them and keep those mistakes out of my repertoire. One of the most important lessons I learned was to be honest in my communications. I had started my marriage with a lie and allowed it to snowball for 18-years. We never discussed money and rarely took time out of our schedules to reconnect and catch up. We allowed our jobs, children, families, friends and money to come between us and discovered when we did come together, we had nothing to say. There is no way I will allow that to happen again.

But, I discovered that my greatest fear was that I would end up a lonely old woman. I read a plethora of self-help books and decided that I would use my dating hiatus to discover myself. I participated in my own self-study: I would participate in a series of events without asking a girlfriend to be my wing-woman and with an attitude that I was on a grand adventure. So, I went on vacations – alone; tried new restaurants – alone; went to parties where I knew only one or two people – alone; and made no plans on weekends when my daughter was at her father's, but instead, spent those Friday, Saturday's and Sunday's – alone. What I discovered was the very important difference between being *alone* and being *lonely*. I had felt lonely in my marriage. Lonely when I attended my former husband's work parties. I was lonely way back in college when I allowed myself to have physical relationships without the benefit of being in a long-term relationship. However, when I was alone in situations I had entered with a cheerful disposition and no expectations, I felt content and re-energized in that "alone-ness" and took great pleasure in meeting new friends, exploring cities and towns I'd never traveled to before. I began to look forward to the simple pleasure of curling up on my daybed with a good book in my apartment on a quiet weekend afternoon or evening: NPR playing on the radio, cooking my favorite foods and savoring a glass of wine. It is at this stage....when we are complete as ourselves that we are able to complement another.

Kudos to those who are able to move on quickly and replace their previous partner without hesitation...I am not that type of person. I prefer to take my time and know that I have confidence in my ability to love someone without barriers before I have any business entering into another marriage. I am very happy with this area of my life: I am neither lonely nor rarely alone.

Lorie Tensen

PATHWAY TO SUCCESS

Lorie Tensen

After obtaining a B.S. in psychology in 2010, I had no clue which direction I wanted to go career wise. I had been a stay-at-home mom for 10-years and my areas of expertise were cooking, cleaning, entertaining and volunteering. It was sobering and quite scary because I knew I only had a couple of years of spousal support remaining and child support that wouldn't even cover the rent. What type of career was out there for a middle-aged woman who was missing a limb and had no real long-term work experience? There weren't a lot of choices that would pay the bills and pad my retirement account. During the next couple of years, I worked as a temp at part-time jobs. At one point, found a full-time position but the pay was less than stellar and it was just a job. There was no joy, no satisfaction, and no hope for the future. Nothing about it that made me look forward to hopping out of bed on Monday mornings! My baby would soon be entering high school and in a blink of an eye, college. As an empty-nester, I would have plenty of time to focus on building a career from the ground floor up and it had to be something I was passionate about. It took a couple of years, but while working part-time at as an operator at a rehabilitation hospital, I discovered my true calling.

Being around fellow amputees had never appealed to me in the past. Why bring attention to my own disability by being around others who were missing arms

146

and legs. No one had referred to me as a "disabled" person and I didn't see me self as having limitations. However, therapy had given me the courage to accept that I did, indeed, have a disability. It didn't mean I was unable to build a successful career, just as it hadn't limited my ability to be a parent. So, I took a part-time position as an operator at a local rehabilitation hospital. I was very familiar with this hospital because it was the same hospital I went to when I needed my prosthesis repaired. I figured with nearly 30-years of life experience, this would be a great fit. Despite the difficult hours and zero opportunity for advancement, I loved my job. I met inspiring patients and their family members who came to the hospital for lengthy stays and for various reasons: some were new amputees; many had brain injuries and spinal injuries. The hospital had a reputation as a stellar rehabilitation facility. As a weekend operator at the main desk, I was privy to the comings and goings of patients and their families at all hours of the day and night. Because many of these patients spent weeks and sometimes months in the hospital, strangers soon became familiar faces I looked forward to seeing during my shifts. Experiencing my own traumatic accident had given me the ability to empathize and soon, stops at my desk became mini therapy sessions. I loved it. I understood the pain and frustration the patients were going through and I had witnessed the helplessness that their loved ones felt in my own family members so many years ago. I listened quietly, provided a shoulder for the many tears that were shed and because I was not a counselor, chose my words with care when asked for words advice. I was good at this. Conversations, whether a brief 10 minutes or the many that lasted for hours energized, rather than drained me. Life coaching was my calling and after coming up against nothing but dead ends, even at the rehabilitation hospital where I worked, I decided to go it alone. I researched the field, trained with the University of Michigan Orthotics and Prosthetics team in Ann Arbor, Michigan and started a business called The 2.1 Advocacy Group. The 2.1 stood for 2 arms, 2 legs, and 1 heart. For those of us with physical disabilities, while we are very well aware of the fact that we are seen as disabled by outsiders, we see ourselves as merely having limitations. Yes, we might have to come up with creative ways to do the things able-bodied persons take for granted, but underneath it all we have the same hopes and dreams and hearts that long for love and acceptance.

My intention for this business was to act as an advocate for those who had experienced trauma in their lives. From my own personal experience, I knew the rocky road that lay ahead of folks and their family members. My mother still talks about not knowing how to prepare me for the challenges I was facing and not having readily available resources or mentors. Not one medical professional offered my parents direction. My parents felt completely alone. They had no clue that I should have received counseling for months – perhaps years – after my accident. They were not advised about how to handle my mental state or my physical requirements. They were not given the tools to guide me from adolescence into adulthood. This was over 30 years ago, of course and thankfully, times have changed. The internet would have provided my family with a plethora of resources to choose from.

What would not have changed, however, was our fear of the unknown. We were never assigned mentors – a family with a child who had experienced limb loss, or, even the wisdom of an adult who had walked a mile in shoes similar to the ones I was now wearing. Who better to talk to than someone who'd walked that path before you? I wanted to use my life experience and act as an advocate, coach and consultant to help these families. A noble career, one I knew I would be an expert at and with the full support of my own prosthetic technician, who I had worked with for 30 years, I started knocking on doors. I quickly found out, however, that the medical community in Grand Rapids wanted nothing to do with me. I was a tiny fish in an enormous sea. Doors were slammed in my face with a resounding BANG and I had to take a giant step back to reevaluate my next step.

By this point in the book, I hope you've come to realize that I am not a quitter! I don't give up easily and if the front door is slammed in my face, I'll try the back door...and maybe even the windows! I had spent too many years of my life settling for second place, with a history of keeping my mouth shut while helping those around me obtain their dreams. No more. I am a goal-setter who's incredibly stubborn and I am no longer willing to settle. The result of being turned away over and over eventually led me to meet the person who would encourage me to write this book and in the midst of our conversation, I discovered a new window of opportunity: I would write my story and turn it into a lifetime career. Even if just one person read my story and knew that I, too, had struggled mentally, emotionally and physically, yet still managed to see the beauty and richness that is my life today and it gave them hope, I would consider myself a success.

TAKING MY HAND OUT OF MY POCKET

Sometime in early 2014, I was fortunate to meet the woman who would become my mentor. We met for coffee one morning for what was supposed to be a meeting about what life was like as an insurance agent. While I had originally intended on earning my living as a consultant, reality has a not-so-subtle way of stepping in and reminded me that my intentions were not paying the bills. I had accepted a position as a Benefits Specialist in the fall of the previous year and despised everything about it with the exception of ensuring customers that they were properly signed up for health insurance benefits and a few of my co-workers. I earned my Producer's license for Life, Accident and Health insurance on my own time and had found it intriguing. I received an inquiry from a Regional Manager of a national insurance agency and after an initial interview with him, took him up on his suggestion to meet a local agent who is one of the most successful agents in the Grand Rapids area. Her name was Maria Erazo.

Maria is a beautiful, successful business woman who owns a flourishing insurance agency and she exudes a zest for life in such a way that I knew immediately upon meeting her that I wanted to approach my career the same way she did. We chatted for a bit about her business and at some point, she asked what my expectations were as a potential insurance agent. After I gave her a brief synapses of my work history, Maria sat back with a puzzled look, crossed her arms, looked me straight in the eye and said: "There's more to your story than what you're telling me." I was a bit taken aback that she had picked up on that and so I explained that I would be crossing into personal history territory if I went deeper into my story and I was hesitant to do so. She said yes, she wanted me to be as open and honest as I could and for some reason, I felt comfortable enough to open up about my life - both past and present.

When I had finished my story, I could see that Maria was visibly moved. She leaned forward in her chair and stated very emphatically: "THIS is what you're passionate about! You have a story to tell and you need to tell it! Telling your personal story is your calling in life and you need to listen to your heart and follow that calling." Then, she asked if I had ever considered writing a book about my life. I had indeed entertained that thought and had made several false starts throughout the years. I knew I had somewhat of a unique story, but I was scared....hesitant to share such intimate stories about my life, stories that still cut to the quick and stories that might reopen old wounds and show my many weaknesses, vulnerabilities and failures. Added to that was my still present fear of being exposed: I'd spent my entire life hiding my hand in my pocket both literally and figuratively and wasn't sure I had the courage to make the fact that I wore a prosthetic public knowledge. Did I really want to see pity in the eyes of my friends? Could I handle answering the inevitable questions that would surely arise? How would my children react – especially my son – because of the very personal story of his birth? How would my family feel...and my mother, dear heavens, my mother. Was she ready for me to tell my story and heaven forbid if anyone took it upon themselves to judge her?

I struggled with all of these questions and spoke with members of my family, but in the end, I knew that this was my life, my story, my decision. I was not about to write anything malicious or salacious. I decided to write the book. Maria had written her own book and is also a successful life coach. She put me in touch with her marketing guru, Mario, and the rest is now history.

What is most important to me about sharing my story and allowing the general public access to my most painful and private moments, is not because I think it might make an interesting read. It is the overwhelming fact that because of a moment in my life 36 years ago, I have been on a journey of self-discovery that will probably continue until the day I die. I have discovered that I am stronger than I ever dreamed. I have endured a traumatic, life-changing experience and I proudly call myself a Survivor. I have been my own harshest critic and the most cutting judge of my character but, on my journey, I have discovered my own personal value and I am finally able to say, with confidence, I am beautiful, lovable and unique.

I know that there are many people who are also on journeys of self-discovery. More likely than not, their journeys are different than mine – their personal stories could be about struggles with sexuality, bullying, addiction, depression, acceptance. My fellow travelers could be strangers and friends, men and women, old and the young and everything in between all of those categories. Their lessons in life are no less painful than mine. Some people have not yet found the courage it takes to share their stories with others...or even with themselves...they keep their hands in their pockets because it's less painful than facing one's demons.

I have chosen to take my hand out of my pocket. In 2014, I chose to change my life inertia, my life trajectory and it is not an easy process, especially at my age. I am in my late 40s...nearly 50 years old. Almost four decades have passed since my accident and it took me a lifetime to finally gather the courage to start living my best life. That meant letting go of the past and using some of those past experiences to affect positive change in my attitude and approach towards life. I made a conscious decision to let go of any lingering bitterness I had towards my former husband and decided to make more of an effort to be civil. I let go of friendships that were toxic: I believe that there is a season for every relationship in your life and when nothing but negativity when you are around someone, it's time to say goodbye. I was no longer willing to settle for any job just to pay the bills: I began focusing on my passion and work full-time turning it into a career. Letting go of my anger, bitterness, negativity and choosing to fill my waking hours with positive thoughts and cheerful energy has indeed changed my life inertia.

This is the message I choose to share with anyone who is willing to listen: no matter what your personal story is and no matter how far along you are on your journey, find the courage to take your hand out of your pocket and know that it is never too late. We must all face our fears and facing those means the difference between living your life to the fullest or standing on the sidelines watching life pass you by.

I am looking forward to the next phase of my life's journey. Writing this book was just the beginning. I am preparing myself for what I hope will be a lifetime of service: sharing my story and offering hope and inspiration to others. I have already been humbled by the stories of personal journeys that people from near and far have chosen to share with me. The 13-year old girl who's right arm was ground to bits in a meat grinder one hot afternoon in August of 1979 could never have imagined those 35-years later, she would have the opportunity to inspire others with her story. I vividly recall my final walk around Willmar wearing a tank top that left both arms exposed. I was mortified and despite the successful walk, immediately covered up upon my return to the OT room. The thought that some day in the future, I would write a book about my story and share it with people as far away as Australia, would have been incomprehensible. I wonder what is next!

Lorie Tensen

THE BEGINNING OF THE END

I have been asked numerous times how I really feel about the events that led up to the accident which caused my lower right arm to be amputated. Here is what I say: I am where I am meant to be in life. Each moment is precious and it is a waste of my time and energy to have regrets. I am truly thankful for every experience I've gone through....and am much more tolerant and wise because of those experiences. I do not dwell on hypothetical questions about how my life would have turned out had I not gone through what I did, after all: I still play piano, still type faster than most people I know and still catch myself considering whether or not I can still tie my shoes with my teeth...I still experienced life as a daughter, sister, wife, mother and friend. My life has continued to be richly blessed.

I end this book with the realizing that there is so much to look forward to! I have reached the fall season of my life, the calendar says that I am approaching my fifth decade and the winter of my life is just around the corner. But, I know I've yet to reach my full potential. My mother is healthy, my siblings and their children are thriving: the next generation of weddings has begun and four great-grandchildren have joined our family tree. My own children continue to move forward with their lives and someday, my family tree will expand, as well. So, I end this story with a question and challenge:

Courage. It's one of my favorite words. Do you have what it takes to change your life's inertia? Are you hiding your "hand" in your "pocket"? Courage: it is time to step out of the shadows of others and live your best life. Courage: make a commitment to yourself and appreciate the value you bring to the table of life. Courage. Take your hand out of your pocket.

Peace

~Lorie

About the Author

The epitome of perseverance, determination, and optimism: Lorie Tensen shares her story of life as a biracial child trans-racially adopted as a baby and growing up in the all-white Minnesota farming community of Brooten in the Midwest by a Dutch, Christian Reformed couple during the race riots of the late 1960's. From losing her arm in a meat grinder at the tender age of 13, struggling with depression and divorce, Lorie, for the first time in her life, opens up and candidly takes you by the hand behind the scenes to inspire, motivate, and share with you how to overcome the adversity in your life so you can achieve joy and victory today!

www.ingramcontent.com/pod-product-compliance
Lightning Source LLC
Chambersburg PA
CBHW070042100426
42740CB00013B/2766